TO THE FARTHEST GULF

The Story of the American China Trade

Elias Hasket Derby (1739-1799), posthumous oil portrait by James Frothingham, early 19th C. Derby is portrayed here at his desk, with a chart and some letters. The larger vessel in the background is his Grand Turk, *the first vessel from New England to visit China. Regarded as America's first millionaire, Derby was unique among Salem's successful merchants for not having gone to sea; he learned the shipping business at the counting house of his father, Richard Derby. His fortune was founded on a fleet of privateers formed during the American Revolution and converted to merchantment after the war. With a fleet of around three dozen ships, Derby spearheaded New England's trade with China, the Philippines, the East Indies and the Baltic. (Peabody Museum of Salem, gift of the Derby family; photograph by Mark Sexton.)*

DOROTHY SCHURMAN HAWES

TO THE FARTHEST GULF

The Story of the American China Trade

Edited and with an Introduction by
JOHN QUENTIN FELLER

THE IPSWICH PRESS
Ipswich, Massachusetts

Publisher's Note

A number of "coffee table" art books and exhibition catalogues dealing with the American China trade have appeared in recent years, but there is very little in print now about the fascinating history of that trade for the general reader, collector, or museum visitor. Our publication of this lively and informative account aims to fill that gap.

Dorothy Schurman Hawes' interest in China began with her residence there as the daughter of Jacob Gould Schurman, U. S. Minister to China, 1921-25, and continued throughout her life, including a decade when her husband was stationed in Shanghai and Beijing as a Marine Corps officer.

Mrs. Hawes' text was originally published in the form of illustrated articles in the *Essex Institute Historical Collections,* of Salem, Massachusetts, in 1941. That text has been altered in a very few places, usually to provide a fuller explanation or identification, to change geographical spellings, or to take note of intervening historical events. In addition, the original selection of illustrations has been expanded by additions from the collections of the Peabody Museum of Salem, the Boston Athenaeum, and Dr. John Quentin Feller, for which we are most grateful.

We are also indebted to the author's son, G. Michael McHugh, for providing biographical and other background information about his mother and her family; to Lindsey G. Brace for invaluable editorial assistance in readying the manuscript for the press; and to David Elliott for his enthusiastic participation at many stages of the project.

THE IPSWICH PRESS
Box 291, Ipswich, Massachusetts 01938

CONTENTS

ILLUSTRATIONS

A description of the cover art will be found at the end of the volume.

INTRODUCTION

by JOHN QUENTIN FELLER

This is the first publication in book form of Dorothy Schurman Hawes' *To the Farthest Gulf.* It originally appeared almost fifty years ago in successive issues of *Historical Collections,* published by the Essex Institute in Salem, Massachusetts. The two-part article was subtitled *Outline of the Old China Trade, 1784-1844,* and the author began by tracing the origins of trade between the Celestial Empire and Europe beginning with Marco Polo's appearance at the court of Kublai Khan in the thirteenth century and the arrival of the Portuguese three centuries later. One of the amazing things about Mrs. Hawes' monograph is that a half century later it is not dated but retains its lively flavor.

To the Farthest Gulf is only one in a series of scholarly studies about the Sino-American trade which have appeared during the past half-century or so. In 1930, Foster Rhea Dulles published his *The Old China Trade,* a slender volume which explored "something of the spirit of adventure and daring which at the close of the Revolution sent the young merchant seamen of the Atlantic seaboard throughout the length and breadth of the Pacific." In a pattern followed closely by Hawes and others, Dulles recounted the premier voyage of *Empress of China* to Canton in 1784 and ended his narrative with the signing of the Treaty of Wanghia between the United States and China in 1844. Indeed, so close are the parallels that one suspects today that it was the Dulles volume which inspired Dorothy Hawes eleven years later and which she included in her "References," or bibliography.

Interest in the China trade flourished during the years after the publication of the Dulles book and the Hawes articles, and during the 1970's and '80's there appeared an outpouring of books, museum catalogs, and articles which culminated in the bicentennial observance of the *Empress of China's* voyage of 1784, with special exhibitions at the New-York Historical Society, the Philadelphia Museum of Art, and the National Portrait Gallery partially satisfying the appetite of collectors and scholars alike. In the catalogs which accompanied these exhibitions, the curators once again seemed to feel restricted to the six decades between 1784 and 1844. *Philadelphians and the China Trade, 1784-1844* was the name of one catalog, while *Adventurous Pursuits: Americans and the China Trade, 1784-1844* described the exhibition at the National Portrait Gallery. Conrad Edick Wright's introductory essay to *New York and the China Trade* covered essentially the same ground, beginning with the *Empress'* voyage and taking the story of the China trade into the 1850's, or just beyond the Treaty of Wanghia. Interestingly, guest-curator David S. Howard included dozens of China trade articles from the period *after* Wanghia, including a number of Canton *famille-rose* porcelains from the late 1860's which I had discussed in my own Peabody Museum catalog, *The Canton Famille Rose Porcelains,* published in 1983, and in a partially-completed four-part series entitled "The Canton famille-rose porcelains," which appeared in *The Magazine ANTIQUES* between 1983 and 1986.

To the Farthest Gulf examines the origins of China's trade with the West with special emphasis given to her European partners in the eighteenth century. The Emperor Ch'ien Lung (1735-1796), like his predecessors and several successors, exhibited a remarkable disdain for the West. Indeed, as Mrs. Hawes commented acidly: "He was totally ignorant of and failed completely to recognize the position and power of western nations." When, for example, King George III sent Lord Macartney's embassy to Jehol in 1793, the Ch'ien Lung emperor chided the English monarch: "It behoves you, O King, to respect my sentiments and to display even greater loyalty in the future so that, by perpetual submission to our throne, you may secure peace and prosperity for your country hereafter." Such verbal disdain, combined with the Chinese insistence on the *kowtow* and foreign complacency, were not inspiring and did little credit to either side, according to Mrs. Hawes.

by John Quentin Feller

The United States did not directly enter the China trade until February 1784, when on General Washington's birthday, *Empress of China* sailed from New York City, reaching Macao in August, before proceeding to Whampoa, the anchorage permitted the "foreign devils" near Canton. *Empress* returned to New York City eight months later with a valuable cargo consisting principally of teas (bohea, hyson, pekoe), silks and nankeens, and some boxes of porcelain.

Before *Empress of China's* return, a second vessel, *Pallas*, arrived at Whampoa and is reputed to have brought back to Baltimore in 1786 a set of china decorated with the insignia of the Society of the Cincinnati, much of which was later purchased by Henry Lee and George Washington. Within the brief space of a half-dozen years, twenty-eight ships had sailed from Baltimore, Philadelphia, New York, Providence, Boston, and Salem. In the years 1818-19, forty-seven American vessels were at the Whampoa anchorage.

American entrepreneurs who engaged in the China trade prior to the signing of the Treaty of Wanghia in 1844 learned, as had their European cousins before them, that a complicated system known as the co-hong was in place to regulate all aspects of the trade. The co-hong was a reference to a cabal of Chinese merchants, thirteen in number, who acted as a buffer between native officials, such as the Viceroy at Canton, and European traders. More importantly, they acted "as guarantors for the good conduct of the foreigners." Although several of the hong merchants, and particularly Houqua, won the respect and admiration of the Americans, the co-hong itself was an archaic, insufferable arrangement. Mrs. Hawes includes the eight regulations governing the trade at Canton which, among other things, forbade foreigners "to pass the night out or to carouse." Another regulation stated: "Neither women, guns, spears, nor arms of any kind can be brought to the factories." Americans and Europeans were admonished that they "must not row about the [Pearl] river in their boats for pleasure."

For those adventurous American businessmen and sea captains who risked their lives and fortunes, if not their sacred honor, in the pursuit of profit, it was incumbent that articles of trade desired by the Chinese be discovered and quickly, for the infant Republic was short on silver coins or specie normally exchanged for Chinese goods by the Europeans. Ginseng, which was found growing wild on American mountains and in the forests, was

iii

highly prized by the Chinese, who believed that its phallus-shaped root was a cure-all and aphrodisiac. Unfortunately, the Chinese market was easily glutted. A little ginseng went a long way.

Mrs. Hawes describes in some detail the importance of furs in the China trade, particularly the pelts of the sea otters and seals which were readily available to those vessels sailing west around the South American horn. Indians in the Pacific Northwest readily traded furs—which brought enormous profits to the Americans at Canton—for guns, nails, rope and other miscellany, but the natives could be unpredictable and treacherous, as the sailors on *Columbia, Boston* and *Tonquin* learned.

Other articles which assumed an importance in the Sino-American trade included bêches-de-mer or sea slugs and birds' nests prized by the Chinese for their soups, as well as fragrant sandalwood which the Chinese made into joss sticks to be burned in their temples. Later, in the decades following the War of 1812 and the explosion of New England's textile industry (fueled in part by the decline in the China trade because of the Embargo of 1807 and the Nonintercourse Act, not to mention the Anglo-American war which lasted two and a half years), American cotton cloth became a trade staple and was used by the Chinese in part to line those wondrous silk embroidered coats, shawls, and table scarves which continued to remain popular in American households throughout the nineteenth century.

In contrast, Americans (and Europeans) imported huge quantities of tea, as well as silks, nankeens, lacquerware, furniture crafted in both Oriental and Occidental styles, elegant fans, the ubiquitous willow-pattern china, and various bric-a-brac. Today, we tend to think of the decorative art objects, I suppose, forgetting that from the very beginning tea, a consumable, accounted for the lion's share of the trade. Actually, most of the nonperishables were part of what has been called "private trade," a practice by which officers and sailors were allotted cargo space according to rank so that they too might profit from an adventurous pursuit. The private trade was encouraged by American ship owners like Elias Hasket Derby as a principle of good business to such an extent that accurate records of the Sino-American trade simply do not exist, and those who rely on ships' papers or bills of lading to ascertain the scope of the trade of the last century are shortsighted.

by John Quentin Feller

The nature of the trade itself made the whole venture risky, and fortunes were made and lost in the process. Robert Morris, a signer of the Declaration of Independence and superintendent of finance during the Revolutionary War, spent three years in debtors' prison because of land and commercial speculation. Others, like Thomas Handasyd Perkins of Nahant, commenting on the vicissitudes affecting trade at the time of the War of 1812, remarked casually: "Embargoes and non-intercourse . . . crossed our path; but we kept our trade with China." Another experienced merchant added merrily: "Tea must be drunk & Silk will be worn, while any female influence remains in Society, & that will be till happy millenium." The eminently successful Robert Bennet Forbes, whose stately home in Milton once housed the Museum of the American-China Trade and later China Trade Museum (now happily conjoined with the Peabody Museum of Salem), put it even more bluntly: "I did not come [to China] for my health."

In *To the Farthest Gulf*, the student of the China trade will meet these and other adventurous souls. Dorothy Hawes introduces the reader to John Ledyard, the Hartford-born American who sailed with Captain Cook on the latter's third and final voyage, and whose stories inspired Philadelphia's Robert Morris and others. Elias Hasket Derby, second son of Salem's Richard Derby, comes to life in Mrs. Hawes' account, which mentions the voyage in 1786 of *Grand Turk*, the first New England vessel to engage directly in the China trade. The town of Salem was enriched and transmogrified through her intercourse with the Chinese, and many of the grand houses which line Chestnut Street are filled with the lure of the exotic. In cities like Providence and Charleston, the best residential sections ran parallel to the waterfront; in Baltimore, even to this day, the neighborhood of Canton with its restored red brick townhouses lies immediately to the north of Harbor Place. The taipans, John Perkins Cushing, long associated with Russell and Co., and Daniel Washington Cincinnatus Olyphant, who singularly opposed the opium trade, join John Jacob Astor, Francis Terranova, and Caleb Cushing in Mrs. Hawes' charming account.

Like Dulles and Hawes, contemporary scholars for the most part have overlooked the fact that what has sometimes been called the "old China trade" did not really end with the Opium War in the late 1830's and Wanghia, but prospered particularly during the 1860's and throughout the '70's. As late as the turn of the century, for example, large quantities of Chinese porcelain were still being imported and advertised in American newspapers. To suggest that Sino-American commerce suddenly diminished after 1844 is to misunderstand what was going on throughout the nineteenth century, especially in the second half. Indeed, this was the very point I argued in my four-part *ANTIQUES* series and in related articles published within the past half-dozen years or so and which, it now seems, has been accepted by most scholars concerned with the Sino-American porcelain trade in particular during the nineteenth century.

Of course it is possible to distinguish between the "old China trade," or rather the mechanics of trade prior to Wanghia, and commercial regulations adopted in 1842 which replaced the system of the co-hongs. Indeed, Dorothy Hawes does precisely this after offering her readers a glimpse of the causes and consequences of the Opium War, whose origins in 1839 were the direct result of China's efforts to stamp out the illegal importation of a controlled substance whose effects on the user were all too obvious.

The exportation of opium to the Celestial Empire during the early years of the last century was a black mark on the commerce between the West and China. As early as 1804, American businessmen engaged in the trafficking of inferior Turkish opium and later carried Indian opium to the Pearl River under a contract arrangement with the British. In 1839, when the Chinese attempted to crush the drug trade, more than twenty thousand opium chests were confiscated from the British and destroyed—a loss of more than nine million dollars or its equivalent in pounds sterling. Trade between China and Britain was suspended and British merchantmen were forced to retreat, first to Macao and then to Hong Kong, until the arrival of British troops more than a year later resulted in a humiliating defeat for the Chinese, who were forced to accept the Treaty of Nanking in 1842, opening up the ports of Amoy, Fuchow, Ningpo and Shanghai. Also, China ceded Hong Kong to the British— which will soon be returned—and paid an indemnity of twenty-one million dollars. More importantly, the Treaty of Nanking expressly ended the co-hong system, or the monopoly of foreign trade at Canton. In this sense, the "old China trade" came to an end in 1842. The Treaty of Wanghia was signed two years later between the United States and China and, while it was a bit more specific on such touchy issues as extraterritoriality, it

by John Quentin Feller

basically confirmed the concessions already exacted by our British cousins.

While Dorothy Hawes' account is informative and lively, it is unfortunate that the author should have ended her history with the Treaty of Wanghia, signed in 1844. The story of the "new China trade" remains to be researched fully and told by another hand at another time. Nonetheless, students of the China trade have benefitted from the publication of "picture books" such as Carl Crossman's critically acclaimed *The China Trade: Export Paintings, Furniture, Silver and Other Objects* (The Pyne Press, 1972) and, more recently, Herbert Schiffer *et al.*, *China for America* (Schiffer Publishing Co., 1980). Jean McClure Mudge's *Chinese Export Porcelain in North America* (Clarkson N. Potter, Inc., 1986) is uneven and contains many mistakes, and the author has devoted barely six pages to the export porcelain *after* Wanghia, thus perpetuating a popular misconception begun by Dulles and repeated by Hawes and others.

The Opium War and subsequent treaties marked the end of an era, what Mrs. Hawes has called "the swan song" of the China trade. But for the United States at least, Wanghia also signified the beginnings of a new, prosperous era in Sino-American trade which peaked during the post-Civil War period and continued until the end of the nineteenth century.

—*John Quentin Feller*

Divitis Indiae usque ad ultimum sinum—"To the farthest gulf of the rich East."

Motto of the town of Salem, Massachusetts

"They sailed where no others dared to go—anchored where no one else dreamed of making a trade."

Nathaniel Hawthorne

"Tea must be drunk & Silk will be worn, while any female influence remains in Society, & that will be till happy millenium."

A China trader

"I did not come to China for my health."

Robert Bennet Forbes

1

THE EUROPEAN FORERUNNERS: VENETIAN, PORTUGUESE, SPANISH, DUTCH, ENGLISH

No sooner had America won her independence than she found herself irresistibly drawn by the magnet which had attracted European nations for the last three hundred years—the fabulous wealth of the Indies.

The fascination which China has always exercised over the Western mind was transmitted gradually, first through Portugal, then Spain and Holland to the whole of Europe, to England and eventually to the young Republic. There was scarcely a household at home or abroad that could not boast of at least a few pieces of Delft ware, copies of delicate Chinese porcelains which familiarized the owners with scenes from the land of lotus and bamboo, of temples and pagodas. Curiosity concerning this little known country increased and was stimulated with each ship returning laden with treasures from the East—silks, tapestries, teas subtly perfumed with jasmine, stones and precious metals—but was never fully satisfied, for Europe knew no more of China than she could learn from Chinese art and craft, and China exhibited no reciprocal curiosity, or even interest, in the strangers from the West.

Geographically, the isolation of China was insured by the desert lands of Mongolia on the north, the massive and elevated table lands of Tibet on the west, and, until the Portuguese discovered the southern sea route, the Indian Ocean and the

China Sea on the south. In the two great surges east and west by the Occident and the Orient, there had been no real contact. Alexander's efforts culminated in the wastes of Central Asia (one may still find the Greek influence in certain Chinese sculptures, notably their statuettes of horses), and the Mongol Horde, spreading disaster and terror in both the East and the West, subsided in Europe almost as quickly as it appeared and in China was absorbed by the Sons of Han in the course of time.

The Great Wall of China, symbol of her isolation for centuries, lies crumbling, a melancholy but still majestic monument to a civilization which flowered three thousand years before the birth of Christ.* Chinese culture, developed within the borders of China proper, owes nothing to the stimulus of outside influence. If from time to time savage and hostile Tartar tribes swept victoriously through the country, they were in the end defeated by a force more potent than physical strength; in a mellow atmosphere of learning and elegance, the Mongols found it easy to forget their tents on the plains for the flowering courtyards of China and to settle complacently into the life of Chinese gentlemen. The amazing thing is that Chinese culture did not stagnate, and it is a lasting tribute to the vigor of the race that unaided it should maintain such a high state. This very fact, however, bred a bigoted disdain for other peoples and a complete indifference to, and a lack of knowledge of, the outside world. For the Chinese there was only one nation under the sun; all other races were considered as tribute-bearing, vassal tribes.

For twelve hundred years the Arabs maintained the chief channel of communication between Europe and the Orient. Through them the costly silks which adorned the women of Rome were brought to the West, and the land from whence they came was known as Serica. In the thirteenth century Kublai Khan ascended the Dragon Throne and it was during his reign that the famous Venetian travelers, the Polos, arrived via the overland route at the court of the great Khan, where they were courteously received and enthusiastically questioned as to the laws and usages of their country. Marco Polo's matchless account of his travels fired the imagination of the West and set Europe

---

* Restoration of parts of the 2500-mile Great Wall has been undertaken in recent years, notably the most accessible section, which is at Badaling, some 50 miles from Beijing.

2

a-dreaming, although his writings at that time were considered the figment of a capricious fancy and earned him the soubriquet of "Marco Milioni." As late as the nineteenth century, English schoolboys were still calling a whopper a "Marco Polo."

Two hundred years elapsed before the light burst, and then Columbus sailed the Atlantic to stumble on the shores of North America instead of finding, as he had hoped, a direct route to the Indies.

The Polos were not the first Europeans to enter China in the thirteenth century. Says Sir Henry Yule, "That a great and civilized country, so-called, existed had already been reported in Europe by Friars Carpini and Rubruquis." People were recovering from the shock of Genghis Khan's thundering Mongol Horde and were beginning to look toward the East with curiosity.

In the sixteenth century the Portuguese arrived in south China by the sea route through the Indian Ocean, but did not at first identify the country with the Cathay of Marco Polo. Close on their heels followed the rest of Europe, bent either on spreading the Gospel or in search of the treasures of Ind. The first Christian envoys to reach Peking* were the Jesuit fathers, Pantoja and Bastien, who suffered various tribulations en route from Macao to the capital via Nanking, but were cordially welcomed by the Emperor, who, although advised by the Board of Rites not to receive them, was delighted with the presents they brought—clocks and other curiosities not seen before in China. Father Ricci was ordained Superior of the Peking Mission, and when he died the Emperor gave grounds and buildings for his interment, the first ecclesiastical property acquired by foreigners in China.

The contributions of the Jesuits were many. Among them were astronomers, mathematicians, geographers and historians. Between 1708 and 1718 the "Maps of China" were made under the direction of Father Tartoux by order of K'ang Hsi, and still standing on the city walls of Peking silhouetted against the sky are the magnificent astronomical instruments designed by Father Verbiest. In 1900, by order of the Kaiser after the Boxer uprising, they were sent to Potsdam to embellish the Orangerie

---

* The Chinese place names used by Mrs. Hawes have been left unchanged, since these forms were in use by the Americans and British during the period covered by this book. The contemporary Pinyin equivalents are shown in italics in the index.

of Sans Souci, but a stipulation of the Treaty of Versailles returned them to their original site. The Jesuits were the agents for imparting knowledge not only to the East but to the West as well; their maps, translations, historical data and accurate information did much to enlighten a wondering Europe.

This order managed to reconcile certain Chinese rites such as ancestor worship with the tenets of Christianity and, while introducing new beliefs, were able to live in harmony with their converts and with the mass of people as well. In 1631 the first Dominican Friars arrived in China and were scandalized by the tolerant attitude of the Jesuits. Chinese rites and the correct translation of the term for God became controversial questions among the members of the Church, and the whole matter was referred to the Pope for a decision. No people are more tolerant than the Chinese in matters concerning religion, but the Emperor K'ang Hsi, fearing that loyalty to the Pope might cause divided allegiance to himself, ordered the Board of Rites to proscribe foreign doctrines throughout the Empire. In 1723 his successor Yung Cheng vehemently denounced Christianity and all Christians, and thus passed the golden age of Jesuit influence in China.

If missionary influence waned, trade was steadily increasing. The first Portuguese arrivals succeeded in establishing friendly relations with the provincial authorities at Canton, but the conduct of the traders who came later was so disgraceful they were driven from the coastal ports. In 1545 the Chinese, incensed with the seizure of women and girls, massacred all the Christians in Ningpo, among them eight hundred Portuguese, and four years afterwards a similar massacre occurred at Ch'uan-chou. The survivors retired to a small island near Macao and from time to time helped the Chinese to drive off pirates who infested the coast. The natives gradually became accustomed to, and no longer feared, the strangers from the West (who had no doubt calmed down after their reverses) and petitioned the Emperor to grant the island of Macao to the foreigners for the purpose of drying their sails and damaged goods. Because of assistance rendered in suppressing pirates and also probably because Macao was a barren rock, the Emperor granted the request, provided a ground rent of five hundred taels a year was paid.*

---

* A tael is equivalent to slightly more than an ounce of silver.

4

Following the Portuguese came Spanish and Dutch traders whose conduct was hardly less reprehensible. The first English vessels arrived in 1635, but the Portuguese had so misrepresented the British character to the Chinese that they were denied the privilege of trade until after a show of force when the Chinese capitulated to their requests. No further attempt to trade was made by the British until 1664. In the first quarter of the eighteenth century an Imperial edict restricted all foreign commerce to the city of Canton—China's attempt to relegate as far from her center of culture as possible the ferocious barbarians who inspired neither liking nor respect, but mistrust because of their incessant plotting, jealousy and violence.

In 1742 the first British man-of-war to appear in Chinese waters, the *Centurion* under Commodore Anson, refused to leave the Pearl River until supplies were provided. A century later S. Wells Williams wrote: "The constant presence of a man-of-war on the coast of China would perhaps have saved foreigners much of the personal vexations and prevented many of the imposts on trade which the history of foreign intercourse exhibits, making it, in fact, little better than a recital of annoyances on the part of a government too ignorant and too proud to understand its own true interests, and recriminations on the part of traders unable to do more than protest against them." He adds: "A mixture of decision and kindness, such as that exhibited by Anson when demanding only what in itself is right, and backed by an array of force not to be trifled with, has always proved the most successful way of dealing with the Chinese."

How the Chinese thought the foreigners should be dealt with was equally if not more high-handed!

China's emperor in the eighteenth century was one of the greatest she has ever known, Ch'ien Lung, who ascended the Dragon Throne in 1735 and abdicated sixty years later at the age of eighty-five. It was during his reign that the first American ships reached Canton. Under his wise rule the people enjoyed great prosperity and peace. His admiration for the teachings of the sages influenced scholars to compile books on their precepts and his reverence for things of the past led to the reconstruction of ancient temples and buildings, among them the Temple of Heaven. It was a period of creative art, of internal accord and contentment throughout the land. The boundaries of the Empire spread to Outer Mongolia and Tibet, to Turkestan and the northern borders of India, to Burma and Annam [Indochina, or

5

Vietnam]. But Ch'ien Lung, so provident in the government of his country and his people, chose to follow the policy of his ancestors in regard to the outside world. He was totally ignorant of and failed completely to recognize the position and power of the Western nations. For centuries China had been so accustomed to subdue or absorb strangers that to allow barbarians within the borders of the Empire, even for the purpose of friendly trade, was a condescension inspired only by the most tolerant broadmindedness! When Ch'ien Lung, with bland complacency, commanded George III of England "tremblingly to obey," and described himself as "swaying the wide world," he did so in all sincerity and earnestness. The "mandate" handed by Ch'ien Lung to Earl Macartney, George III's ambassador, who came to Peking to seek more favorable trade relations, is couched as follows:*

You, O King, live beyond the confines of many seas, nevertheless impelled by your humble desire to partake of the benefits of civilization you have dispatched a mission respectfully bearing your memorial. Your envoy has crossed the seas and paid his respects at my court on the anniversary of my birthday. To show your devotion you have also sent offerings of your country's produce. . . As to your entreaty to send one of your country's nationals to be accredited to my Celestial Court and to be in control of your country's trade with China, this request is contrary to all usage of my dynasty and cannot possibly be entertained. . . Peking is nearly two thousand miles from Canton, and at such a distance what possible control could any British representative exercise? . . . Swaying the wide world I have but one aim in view, namely to maintain a perfect governance and to fulfill the duties of the State: strange and costly objects do not interest me. If I have commanded that the tribute offerings sent by you, O King, are to be accepted, this is solely in consideration for the spirit which prompted you to send them from afar. . . It behoves you, O King, to respect my sentiments and to display even greater loyalty in the future so that, by perpetual submission to our throne, you may secure peace and prosperity for your country hereafter.

In a further mandate:

Yesterday your Ambassador petitioned my ministers to memorialize me regarding your trade with China, but his proposal is not consistent with our dynastic usage and cannot be entertained. Hitherto all European nations, including your own country's barbarian merchants,

---

* Quoted in E. Backhouse and J. O. P. Bland, *Annals and Memoirs of the Court of Peking.*

have carried on their trade with the Celestial Empire at Canton. Such has been the procedure for many years, although our Celestial Empire possesses all things in prolific abundance and lacks no product within its own borders. There was therefore no need to import the manufacture of outside barbarians in exchange for our own produce. But as the tea, silk and porcelain which the Celestial Empire produces are absolute necessities to European nations and to yourselves, we have permitted, as a signal mark of favor, that foreign 'hongs' should be established at Canton, so that your wants might be supplied and your country thus participate in our beneficence.

Earl Macartney also petitioned for the privilege of trade at other ports—Ningpo, Chusan and Tientsin—but the opening of these ports was refused on the grounds that there were no arrangements for foreign intercourse, no "hongs" and no interpreters. The request for a small island near Chusan and a site near Canton where foreign merchants might reside and repositories be built was likewise denied, and the reduction of duties would not be considered. Ch'ien Lung made it clear, too, that he would not tolerate the dissemination of Christianity throughout his Empire and ended his mandate with the injunction, "Tremblingly obey and show no negligence."

The early history of foreign intercourse is not inspiring and does little credit to either side. The buccaneer adventurers of the sixteenth and seventeenth centuries may have brought upon themselves the restrictions which were placed upon them; on the other hand the Chinese had no conception of international law which had long been established in Europe. Their theory was, "The barbarians are like beasts and not to be ruled on the same principles as citizens. Were anyone to attempt controlling them by the great maxims of reason it would tend to nothing but confusion. The ancient kings well understood this and accordingly ruled the barbarians by misrule; therefore to rule barbarians by misrule is the true and best way of ruling them."

There are many who have argued that surely a great nation has the right to isolate herself if that be the desire of her people. Rodney Gilbert, in refuting this argument, writes: "Commerce is like water, seeking its natural levels over any obstructed course and wearing away obstructions as inevitably as water. . . It is futile to discuss the moral character of the phenomenal tidal movement in world trade that scattered ships, men and their goods broadcast over the globe in the fifteenth, sixteenth and seventeenth centuries, bringing them into contact, and often conflict, with whole races that had been immune theretofore against such visitations."*

In spite of the attitude of the Court at Peking, foreign merchants continued coming to Canton. They submitted to the rigid restrictions which made them voluntary prisoners in the small and uncomfortable area allotted to them and endured every discomfort, even indignity, so great was the value of the tea and silk cargoes annually exported from the country. An anonymous memorial to the Emperor advised him that, "Inquiries have served to show that foreigners, if deprived for several days of the tea and rhubarb of China, are afflicted with dimness of sight and constipation of the bowels to such a degree that life is endangered." The Chinese firmly believed this to be true as year after year the merchants arrived to make their fortunes. A fortunate trader might retire at the age of thirty-five or forty with an income for life.

The Emperor's representative at Canton was the Viceroy under whom were a number of provincial officials, all obliged to purchase their way to the offices they held. The Viceroy's great concern was to forward sufficient revenue to Peking while lining his own pockets and to a lesser degree those of his associates without strangling trade altogether. Imposts were high, but, with the usual Chinese adroitness, both native and foreign merchants were kept in a state of harmony most of the time. Between the officials and foreigners stood the "co-hong," a body of Chinese merchants, limited to thirteen, who were responsible for anything concerning trade. These men were the only persons authorized to deal with the barbarians from across the seas; it was their duty to regulate prices and to act as guarantors for the good conduct of the foreigners. In accordance with the laws of the Empire the co-hongs were forced to endure official wrath as well as the complaints of Europeans, and though their position does not seem enviable there must have been ample remuneration, for in one case an entrance fee of two hundred thousand taels was paid for the privilege of becoming a member. A bond of friendship founded on mutual interests existed between the foreigners and the co-hong, and as long as there was no official interference trade continued smoothly and amicably.

Canton, or as the Chinese called it, the "City of Rams," was founded two hundred years before the birth of Christ. Foreign

* Rodney Gilbert, *The Unequal Treaties.*

trade made it a city of wealth and luxury and the most important place in China outside of Peking. Its population was estimated at over one million inhabitants and it was ten miles in circumference. Europeans, however, were not allowed to enter the city proper, but were compelled to live outside the walls in the suburbs where their factories—narrow buildings of two or three stories with a parade ground in front—faced the river. This whole area was not more than a quarter of a mile square, but here they were confined and were not allowed to leave the grounds either by land or water, except very occasionally under the supervision of a Chinese guide. No foreign women were allowed to disembark from any ship, a regulation in force to prevent "outer barbarians" from becoming permanent residents of the Celestial Empire.

A British captain once took his wife to Canton disguised as a cabin boy. While he was entertaining at dinner one very warm evening his lady threw open her shirt collar and leaned back to drink, which caused considerable excitement among the Chinese attendants. One of them beckoned the captain aside to inform him that the person he supposed a man was in truth a woman because there was no Adam's apple. The captain immediately ordered his barge to be manned, armed, and brought alongside, put his wife out a porthole, and started the boat for Macao. Mandarins guarding the ship pursued with all haste, but the Englishmen were able to escape and arrived safely at the island.

All ships were required to stop at Macao, the gateway to Cathay, to receive a "chop" or permit, before they were allowed to proceed upriver to the anchorage at Whampoa, twelve miles below the city of Canton, where they were moored. The sailors lived on board their vessels, but were allowed to visit the factories in small groups, or to amuse themselves on shore at the anchorage where settlements catering to their tastes had grown up. In the height of the season there might be from two to three thousand men, and they were no doubt a considerable worry both to the Chinese authorities and to their own captains.

The eight regulations governing trade at Canton were as follows:

1. All vessels of war are prohibited from entering the Bogue [the mouth of the Pearl River, a corruption of the Portuguese "Bocca Tigris"].
2. Neither women, guns, spears, nor arms of any kind can be brought to the factories.

3. All river pilots and ships' compradores must be registered at the office of the Tung-che (assistant magistrate) at Macao. That one will also furnish each one of them with a license, or badge, which must be worn around the waist. He must produce it whenever called for. All other boatmen and people must not have communication with foreigners unless under the immediate control of the ship's compradore; and should smuggling take place the compradore of the ship engaged in it will be punished.

4. Each factory is restricted for its service to eight Chinese (irrespective of the number of occupants), say two porters, four water carriers, one person to take care of goods and one merchant.

5. Foreigners must not row about the river in their boats for pleasure. On certain holidays the barbarians may visit the Flower Gardens and the Honam Joss House, but not in droves of over ten at a time and accompanied by a linguist. They shall not be allowed to pass the night out or to carouse. Should they do so, then, when the next holiday comes they shall not be permitted to go out.

6. Foreigners are not allowed to present petitions. If they have anything to represent, it must be done through the co-hong merchants.

7. Co-hong merchants are not to owe debts to foreigners. Smuggling goods to and from the city is prohibited.

8. Foreign ships arriving with merchandise must not loiter about outside the river; they must come direct to Whampoa. They must not rove about the bays at pleasure and sell to rascally natives goods subject to duty, that these may smuggle them, and thereby defraud his Celestial Majesty's revenue.

The first American ship to reach Canton sailed up the Pearl River in 1784; by 1790 twenty-eight vessels had made the journey. The China trade played an important part in the development of the United States not only because of duties which enriched the treasury, nor because it was better to be known abroad as an American rather than a New York or Boston man, but because of a far more lasting effect on American life. The trade was the means of bringing to Americans new ideas and a consciousness of the world outside. Canton, Java, the Straits, the Cape, Más Afuera, Owhyee [as Hawaii was then sometimes styled], and the Marquesas became names as familiar to everyone as the names of the streets in the bustling port towns where the wharves were lined with graceful East Indiamen. The search for commodities in the Canton market led Yankee mariners to the farthest regions of the globe, to the then little-known, rugged and forbidding shores of the northwest coast, to the sun-bathed islands of the Pacific. An empire followed in their wake. As

Dr. Stassa

2881575   519

549 E 72 St

830 AM (830)

Whampoa Anchorage, c. 1845, by Youqua (active 1840-70). In this panoramic view from Dane's Island, American and British ships are shown anchored in Whampoa Reach. In the background is Whampoa Island, with its warehouses, tower and distinctive pagoda. (Collection of Charles Getchell, Hamilton, Mass.)

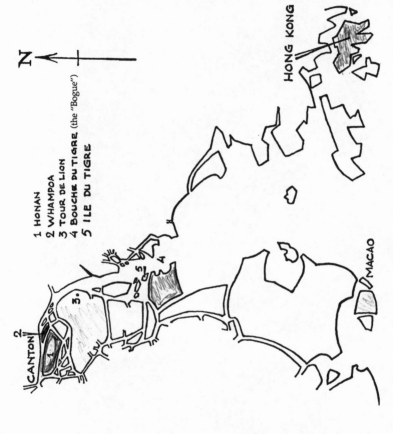

1 HONAN
2 WHAMPOA
3 TOUR DE LION
4 BOUCHE DU TIGRE (the "Bogue")
5 ILE DU TIGRE

Map showing approaches to Canton and Whampoa, in relation to Macao and Hong Kong. (Peabody Museum of Salem.)

the trade grew, the need for faster ships was felt and the clippers were developed. They were designed to outdistance any other ships afloat and they did, but their reign was short-lived, scarcely twenty years, before they were superseded by steam vessels. In their heyday, the American clippers, their sails straining, were second to none in the incredible races from Canton to Liverpool.

The influence of the China trade is still reflected in New England, in the architecture of the old houses with their high balconies where the merchants might look out to sea and watch for the return of their ships; in the Canton china, the shawls and bits of ivory that yet remain. American pioneers of the sea were responsible as much as the frontiersmen for the development of the United States and because of them our interest in the Far East has never waned. Further it is through the old tales of the mariners, an atmosphere created by them, an aura born in the past, that we still see China today. The ancient dragon, awakened and disturbed by the intrusion of unwanted barbarians, may have fled, an age-old Empire become a modern Republic [and then a Communist state], but the conception of China in many western minds often remains a network of half-remembered stories and preconceived ideas.

2

THE ADVENTUROUS JOHN LEDYARD

Bohea, Hyson, Souchong, Congou, Pekoe—although Americans liked their tea, they refused to drink it if the fragrant leaves were imported in British bottoms. Was there not the Boston Tea Party at the expense of the Honorable British East India Company? Shocked as this august body of merchants may have been at the time their cargoes were thrown overboard, they were doubtless more so twenty years later when their American competitors started underselling them in the great marts of the world.

Hardly had Washington's ragged army marched home to put away their uniforms and lay down their muskets than they turned their thoughts to the problem of rehabilitation. Merchants considered ports where they might trade, for their ships were lying idle and sailors wandered the streets. Commerce with the West Indies was stopped after the Revolution; with Europe and Africa it was impractical and with South America contraband, so there was no place to turn except toward Asia. Americans knew from the British that there was a market in Canton for foreign goods, especially for ginseng, a root found growing wild in the northeastern states which was used by the Chinese for medicinal purposes and was highly valued as a restorative of virility. It had already been proved there was a market at home for Chinese teas and silks. This knowledge, plus the reports of a young man from Connecticut, John Ledyard, who sailed with Captain Cook, were causes which led to the development of the East India trade. Ledyard saw skins picked up from the Indians on the northwest coast for less than nothing sell for a hundred dollars each in Canton. He returned home to urge the merchants of New York and Philadelphia to look to the Orient for their profits.

John Ledyard was born in Groton in 1751 and died thirty-seven years later in Africa. He was educated at Dartmouth with the idea of becoming a missionary to the Indians, but left college before completing the course. He then studied theology, though these studies lasted but a short time, for the clergy turned down his application for candidate. John had often heard his grandfather speak of wealthy family connections in London, so he decided to sail for England with the hope that his cousins would help him start on a career. Soon after he arrived, he called at the family residence where he was met by the son of the house who refused to believe either his story or the proofs of his identity. Ledyard, always high tempered, left in a rage and although later apologies and presents of money were offered, he refused to accept either.

The journey to London, however, bore fruit. It was there that Ledyard met the great navigator, Captain Cook, who was preparing for his third and last voyage and who was so impressed with the young American's appearance and manner that he enlisted him in his service with the rank of corporal of Marines. The expedition, consisting of the two ships *Resolution* and *Discovery*, proceeded around the Cape of Good Hope, crossed the Pacific and at length arrived at Nootka Sound on the northwest coast of America. Ledyard wrote of the region:

> The light in which this country will appear most to advantage respects the variety of its animals, and the richness of their furs. They have foxes, sables, hares, marmosets, ermines, weazles, bears, wolves, deer, moose, dogs, otters, beavers, and a species of weazle called the glutton. The skin of this animal was sold at Kamchatka for sixty rubles, which is near twelve guineas. We purchased here about fifteen hundred beaver, besides other skins, but had no thought at the time of using them to any other advantage than converting them to the purpose of clothing, but it afterwards happened that the skins which did not cost the purchaser sixpence, sold in China for one hundred dollars. Neither did we purchase one quarter part of the beaver and other furs we might have done, and most certainly should have done, had we known of meeting the opportunity of disposing of them to such an astonishing profit.

13

Captain Cook commanded Ledyard to explore the nearby woods where he discovered thirty Russians, subjects of the Empress Catherine, trading with the Indians. When the Cook expedition returned home, great public interest was aroused in England, and Catherine, fearing she might meet with competition in her imperial outpost, determined to strengthen her claims and, for that purpose, sent out two ships under Captain Billings, formerly one of Cook's men.

When Ledyard returned home, he attempted to inspire the merchants with his own enthusiasm for the northwest coast and what he was sure were its unlimited possibilities. Robert Morris of Philadelphia at first encouraged him, going so far as to commission him to find a ship, and although a vessel, the *Empress of China*, was purchased, the plan fell through. In New York, Ledyard was considered an impractical, even a wild visionary of somewhat unbalanced mind, and because his efforts met with ill success in his own country he decided to go to Europe. In Cadiz he learned that a ship of seven hundred tons had been fitted out on the Thames and commissioned by the Empress of Russia for a voyage to the hinterland of America.

"You see," he wrote bitterly, "the business deserves the attention I have endeavored and am still striving to give it; and had Morris not shrunk behind a trifling obstruction I should have been happy, and America would at this moment be triumphantly displaying her flag in the most remote and beneficial regions of commerce. I am tired of vexations." Further, "The flame of enterprise I kindled in America terminated in a flash that bespoke little foresight or resolution to my patrons. Perseverance was an effort of understanding which twelve rich merchants were incapable of making."

This extract from one of Ledyard's letters shows how resentful he was toward the American merchants, Robert Morris in particular, but at that time the merchants were not ready for such an undertaking; they were seeking, rather, a safe and reasonably profitable trade than sudden wealth from a land about which little was known except that its inhabitants were savage Indians. Yet one can understand and sympathize with Ledyard's chagrin; time after time he seemed within reach of success in an undertaking the profits of which he felt were assured, only to have his aspirations dashed to the ground. He referred to himself as the "sport of the accident."

Ledyard left Spain for Paris where he met Thomas Jefferson, the American minister to France. Jefferson was much impressed with Ledyard's views and was himself convinced that the large portion of the country outside the United States, separated by no barrier of nature, must eventually become part of the growing nation, and in this conviction originated the journey of Lewis and Clark overland to the Pacific Ocean. While he was in Paris, Ledyard also became acquainted with John Paul Jones, who was there in connection with the famous capture of the *Serapis*. Jones was greatly interested in descriptions of the northwest coast and the two men decided to outfit ships for an expedition to collect furs for sale in Canton where they would reload with teas and silks, but this plan, as in the case of Ledyard's other attempts, failed to materialize because of lack of money and government backing.

From Paris, Ledyard went to London and, under the patronage of Sir Joshua Banks and other gentlemen, a subscription was raised to send him across Siberia to America. His efforts in this direction were frustrated by the Empress Catherine's order to put him under arrest—a step taken to assure her own interests, but excused on the grounds the journey was so dangerous she feared the "courageous American might die!" He was sent back to London and once more engaged by Sir Joshua Banks, this time to lead an expedition into Africa where he succumbed to an illness in his thirty-eighth year.

During his life, John Ledyard suffered reverses which would have discouraged most men, but he never gave up hope of one day seeing his fondest dream come true—an established trade with the northwest Indians and for himself a "small degree of honest fame" for his efforts. It was he who first saw the tremendous value of furs which could be obtained for little from the trappers, and he was the first American to propose voyages to the northwest coast as a mercantile enterprise. Although he died before his aim could be fulfilled, he did ignite the fuse and it was not long before his dream became an accomplished fact.

3

THE *EMPRESS OF CHINA* AND THE LAUNCHING OF THE AMERICAN CHINA TRADE

Influenced by Ledyard's reports, necessitated by poverty, and because by nature the men of New England were shipbuilders and mariners, Americans took to the sea in search of trade and capital. The honor of being the first ship to sail from America to Canton goes to the *Empress of China*, owned jointly by Robert Morris and a group of New York merchants represented by Daniel Parker. Morris wrote to his friend John Jay, "I am sending some ships to China in order to encourage others in the adventurous pursuit of commerce." This was the vessel on which Ledyard had hoped to sail, taking furs for the Canton market, but instead of furs, the cargo consisted of ginseng, cordage, wine, lead, iron and a few Spanish dollars. Captain Green was in command and under him Mr. Peter Hodgkinson, the second captain. In the ship's company were forty-two men, including a surgeon, carpenters, a cooper, a gunner, and boys. The measurement was three hundred and sixty tons, less than one one-hundredth the size of twentieth-century Atlantic liners. The *Empress of China* sailed from New York on Washington's birthday, 1784, saluted the grand battery with thirteen guns, received twelve in return, and thus launched began her long journey to the Orient and American trade with China was inaugurated.

No one could then have realized how important this trade was to become in American life. The ship's owners believed there would be a profit, but not one of them dreamed of the lucrative returns the China trade was to bring , nor the influence it was to exert. The *Empress of China* left New York without fanfare. The men who sailed with her did so because of the need for something to do. Many of them were penniless, in debt even, after the Revolution.

In addition to the officers and crew there were two supercargoes in charge of the commercial interests of the voyage, Major Samuel Shaw of Boston and his friend, Mr. Thomas Randall, both former officers in the American army during the Revolution. Major Shaw had been aide-de-camp to General Knox, commander of the artillery, and served with distinction throughout the war; he was highly thought of by his superior officers and has been described by contemporaries as a man of refinement and education, with a high degree of honor, an agreeable companion, generous and of sound judgment. His *Journal*, relating his experiences on the *Empress of China* and subsequent voyages, is by far the best account written by an American of the existing trade conditions in China and India and is an invaluable source of information concerning the East India trade. On their second expedition, Shaw and Randall bore the titles of consul and vice-consul, respectively, at Canton, the first American officials east of the Cape.

The *Empress of China* sailed from New York to Port Praya on the island of São Tiago, where she remained for six days until her upperworks could be repaired While there Shaw, Randall and Captain Green saw much of the island and paid a call on the commandant of the fort, a Portuguese, who, after he had received a five dollar anchorage fee, hinted that a "compliment" for himself would not be out of order. Other visitors to the island had reported that the Portuguese were great rogues and sharp in barter. In the harbor lay a French brig crowded with naked blacks bought for five crowns a head in Senegal and doomed for market at the Cape, where the demand was great. Before sailing, Captain Green took on board a plentiful supply of water, fruit and livestock.

From São Tiago, the *Empress of China* proceeded south, rounded the Cape and on July 17th arrived at the Straits of Sunda, in the Java Sea, where she came upon two French ships at anchor, the *Fabius* and the *Triton*. The former was carrying cannon and supplies for the Dutch at Batavia, while the latter was bound for Canton, under the command of Captain d'Ordelin. In the course of calls between ships, the captain of the *Fabius*

17

told the Americans that he had fought under de Grasse at Chesapeake and had been at the surrender of the British forces to the American and French at Yorktown, and M. d'Ordelin gave them the news that Lafayette had received the order of the American Society of the Cincinnati, an honor with which all France was much pleased. Captain Green decided to sail for Macao in company with the French captain who had already made the trip eleven times, but before weighing anchor a garden of oats, corn, beans, peas and potatoes was planted on the uninhabited Mew Island and the gentlemen of the two ships toasted this undertaking in Madeira and champagne.

On the 24th of August they reached Macao, where the Americans were entertained by the French and Swedish consuls and where Major Shaw took the opportunity to distribute copies of the treaties existing between the United States and friendly European nations. On the 25th, having received a "chop," and with a Chinese pilot on board, the *Empress of China* saluted the *Triton* and set sail for Whampoa, where she arrived three days later, six months out from New York, without mishap and with all hands in good health.

The Pearl River has been the subject of many descriptions, both in writing and in painting; there were few who were not impressed with the vivacious scene and the variegated colors. From its banks on either side rose low, wooded hills while the flats were thickly planted with fruit trees—peach, orange and plantain. Like a city moving slowly, it supported a floating population, over eighty-four thousand, many of whom scarcely ever set foot on land, and its streams and canals were more densely thronged, even, than the streets of Canton. Officers appointed by the government regulated its traffic and controlled the people who sought a livelihood from its waters, who knew no other home than their floating craft.

Along it flowed carrying boats of every description: egg-boats so low a person could scarcely stand up in them; sampans crowded with river men and women and babies with blocks of wood tied to their backs to keep them from drowning should they fall overboard, packed with chickens, pigs and food placed indiscriminately on the small deck space. Vendors and barbers in search of customers darted to and fro among the bigger boats and fortune tellers and theatrical performers advertised their wares in sing-song voice. Gentle waves lapped the sides of flower boats where graceful courtesans, bedecked in jewels, awaited the pleasure of the mandarins. Officials' boats decorated in scarlet bobbed gaily along the banks, while huge salt junks and junks of war flying martial banners moved majestically up and down. The whole scene was a strange medley of luxury and poverty, of the mysterious and the prosaic, of every kind of coarseness and of the greatest magnificence.

One young sailor wrote in his log, "I was happy as any person ever was to see anything. I scarcely believed I was so fortunate as really to be in China. As we sailed up the river I would cast my eyes from side to side: the thoughts and ideas I had pictured to my mind of it were not lessened in brilliancy, rather increased: the immense number of buildings that extended as far as the eye could reach; their fantastic shapes and gaudy colors; their trees and flowers so like their paintings, and the myriads of floating vessels; and above all the fanciful dresses and gaudy colors of their clothes, all serve to fix the mind of a stranger, upon his first arrival."

"Chops" issued at Macao were countersigned at the Bogue Forts, and, if the mandarin came on board to inspect the vessel, a bottle of wine was opened in his honor. As the *Empress of China* advanced slowly upstrean carrying the first American flag to be seen in those waters, she was greeted with salutes from the foreign fleet at anchor along the shore, their tall spars, rising above the junks pressing in on them. Small boats were sent out to greet the newcomers; the French helped the vessel anchor at a good berth, the Danes and Dutch sent officers to call, and the British an officer to welcome the flag in a new corner of the world. The calls were returned.

"On board the British," wrote Major Shaw, "it was impossible to avoid speaking of the late war. They allowed it to have been a great mistake on the part of their nation—were happy it was over—glad to see us in this part of the world—hoped all prejudices would be laid aside, and added that, let England and America be united, they might bid defiance to all the world." This friendly attitude was later considerably modified by order of the British East India Company, whose directors grew seriously alarmed at the increasing proportions of American commerce in China.

4

THE CHINESE TRADING SYSTEM: CANTON FACTORIES AND CO-HONGS

Of the foreign trade at Canton the most important by far was the British and next to it the Dutch; Portuguese and Spanish trade were steadily declining, while the Imperialists (the Austrians) had a company, but it was expected to close at any minute. The Swedes and Danes, as well as the French, made their profits from smuggling tea into England until Parliament commuted the duty on that luxury. Before the arrival of the Americans there was no such thing as free trade; Chinese as well as European commerce was subject to the monopolistic system—the foreigners had companies backed by their governments and the Chinese dealt through the Yeung Hong Sheung, or Foreign Associated merchants, known as the co-hong. The British East India Company had received its charter from Queen Elizabeth in 1600, and the Crown, vitally interested in its success, refused to allow competition from independent traders. It was an establishment of London merchants who were responsible for turning a commercial route into the world's greatest modern empire. The company had a permanent organization at Canton headed by a Select Committee of Supercargoes, it dominated the home market, although the sale of tea and other merchandise was carefully defined by law, and it controlled the "country trade," that is, the trade between India and China. Its trademark was so well known it was not considered necessary to examine goods bearing it.

The friendly interest of the Europeans was of great help to the Americans in expediting their introduction into the Chinese system of doing business. The British, overlooking the "late war," and as yet with no inkling that the American free trade was to put their powerful East India Company out of commission, were most cordial. The French, still feeling the Americans more or less their protegés, not only insisted that Major Shaw and Mr. Randall stay in their factory, but helped to establish the American factory. These factories, so-called, were not places of manufacture but were used as residences and warehouses by the foreign merchants. The words "factory" and "hong" were practically interchangeable. Each factory or hong had a particular designation. Thus, the Austrian was the "Twin Eagle Hong," the British the "Hong that Insures Tranquillity" and the American received the title of the "Hong of Extensive Fountains" as well as the "Flowery Flag Hong."

Two streets ran through the factory area, China Street and Hog Lane, the former lined with silk and antique shops while the latter abounded in grog shops where the the wary Chinese waited for sailors, got them drunk and then robbed them. Hog Lane was the scene of countless brawls which caused difficulties between the foreigners and the Chinese merchants and authorities. Facing China Street from the north stood an extensive and handsome series of buildings known as Consoo House, the council hall of the factories, which was the property of the co-hong merchants and was maintained always in spotless order by funds appropriated for this purpose. This building was used for discussions pertaining to trade and it was here that the taipans, or heads of houses, met the Chinese merchants to talk over old or new regulations or the revision of duty. It was here, too, that the infrequent cases of bankrupcy or other pecuniary troubles were settled.

Before a foreigner could transact any business it was necessary to secure a Chinese merchant to act as guarantor for his ship. In the event no individual would accept this office, either because the cargo did not seem profitable or because the ship's funds were insufficient, the co-hong as a body were obliged to assume the responsibility. In the case of the *Empress of China*, Pwankeiqua became security merchant and thus bound himself as liable to the authorities for the conduct of the Americans. (The suffix "qua" was a term of respect equivalent to the English "sir.")

In 1784, the members of the co-hong numbered eight. This body of merchants possessed great powers and no other merchant in Canton was allowed business dealings with the foreigners unless under their chop. They were accountable to the authorities for any infringement of regulations on the part of the outer barbarians and were the intermediators between the government officers and the Europeans, who were not permitted to address any communication to the officials except through a member of the co-hong and then only in the form of a respectful petition. The commercial character of these merchants was high and their integrity taken for granted, as many Americans and others have testified. But of the shopkeepers and small merchants that could not be said. They were adept in the practice of chicanery, and nothing was too much trouble for them as long as they could make a few extra coppers on a sale. They were past masters in such tricks as stuffing ducks with pebbles to make them weigh more or blowing water into fruits to make them seem larger.

Many of the co-hong, notably the famous Houqua, made tremendous fortunes. (It has been estimated that Houqua was worth twenty-six million dollars at the time of his death.) Others suffered banishment, even death, for incurring the displeasure of the Viceroy. They were all compelled to pay huge taxes, ostensibly for the relief of the poor, for repairing dams, or other civic projects, but most of the duties levied went to enrich the Imperial exchequers and very little to alleviate the burdens of the masses or to improve the community.

The following conversation took place between Houqua and a foreign friend who had come to see him:

"Well, Houqua, have you any news today?"

"Have got too muchee bad news. Hwang Ho (Yellow River) have spillum too muchee."

"Mandarin have come to see you?"

"He no see my. He sendee me one piece chop. He come tomollo. He wantchee my two lac dolla." (A lac was worth one hundred thousand dollars.)

"You pay how much, Houqua?"

"My pay fitty, sikky tousand so."

"But suppose he no contentee?"

"Suppose he number one no contentee, my pay one lac."

After Houqua, Pwankeiqua was the second most prominent member of the co-hong and was particularly popular with the

22

View of foreign factory site, Canton, c. 1830-40, by Sunqua (active 1830-70). Canton was already a major port when Arab merchants settled there in the seventh century. Once China's second city and largest port, Canton held an imperial monopoly on foreign trade from 1715 to 1840. Western merchants were confined to the small area seen in this view. (Peabody Museum of Salem, gift of Mrs. Alfred Vincent Kidder; photograph by Mark Sexton.)

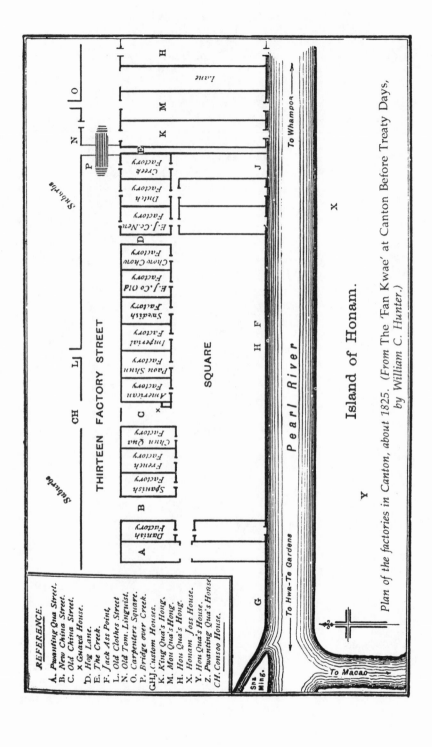

Plan of the factories in Canton, about 1825. (From The 'Fan Kwae' at Canton Before Treaty Days, by William C. Hunter.)

REFERENCE.

A. Pwanting Qua Street.
B. New China Street.
C. Old China Street.
× Guard House.
D. Hog Lane.
E. The Creek.
F. Jack Ass Point.
L. Old Clothes Street.
N. Old Tom. Linguist.
O. Carpenters Square.
P. Bridge over Creek.
G,H,J. Custom Houses.
K. King Qua's Hong.
M. Mou Qua's Hong.
H. Hou Qua's Hong.
X. Honam Joss House.
Y. Hou Qua's House.
Z. Pwanting Qua's House
C.H. Consoo House.

THIRTEEN FACTORY STREET

Danish Factory
Spanish Factory
French Factory
Chun Qua Factory
American Factory
Paou Shun Factory
Imperial Factory
Swedish Factory
E.I.Co Old Factory
Chow Chow Factory
E.I.Co. New Factory
Dutch Factory
Creek Factory

Suburds

Lane

SQUARE

Pearl River

Island of Honam.

To Whampoa

To Hwa-Te Gardens

To Macao

Sn̄ & Ming.

Americans. At one time he paid five hundred thousand dollars to the authorities for the privilege of retiring, but when a new Viceroy arrived in Canton he was ordered to resume his office as head of the co-hong. Both he and Houqua owned large estates across the river near the Honam temple and both entertained foreigners in their beautiful gardens which were laid out with fish ponds connected with "airy and fairy-like bridges" and were shaded with palm, orange and other fruit trees. Pwankeiqua, the oldest partner in the co-hong, was held in great regard as a man of letters and because of honors conferred by the Emperor was entitled to three flagpoles with the Imperial flags in front of his residence. In 1819, he was made a member of the Massachusetts Agricultural Society. He died in 1824, leaving an estate of ten million dollars.

"Boston traders," wrote Samuel Eliot Morison, "acquired an esteem for the Chinese character which has endured to this day." There are numerous stories of Houqua's generosity. On one occasion he tore up a promissory note for seventy-two thousand dollars owed him by an American who was anxious to get home but would not leave Canton because he could not pay his debt. Houqua asked him to call. "You and I," said the Chinese, "number one ollo good flen. You belong honest man only no got chance." He called for the note and destroyed it. "Just now have settee counter. You go home, please." On another occasion Houqua accepted the consignment of an American ship having on board a large amount of quicksilver, the price of which was much depressed at Canton. As the season advanced the captain decided he could wait no longer and must close the sale of his quicksilver, although the proceeds would bring him enough to purchase only a small cargo of teas. The transaction was "putee book" and Houqua said to the captain, "Ollo flen, you shall have full cargo, you pay me next voyage, you no trub'." In the meantime, the price of quicksilver advanced sharply owing to a sudden demand in the north and just as the American ship was about to leave, Houqua informed the captain he had cancelled on his books the first purchase and had credited the account with the price of the day. This generous act made it possible for the captain to sail for home with a full cargo all paid for and made a difference in his profits of thirty thousand dollars.

The co-hong was responsible for the behavior of all employees in the factories, and no Chinese could offer his services without recommendation of one of the merchants. To run a factory it was necessary to engage a compradore to supply provisions for both factory and ship. This agent collected "squeeze" on all articles furnished and if the ship were small received, besides, a hundred and fifty taels. Next in importance to the compradore came the linguist, who acted as interpreter. The term "linguist" seems a peculiar misnomer, for no Chinese spoke any foreign language and could mimic parrot-like but a few words picked up from the sailors. These, intermingled with Chinese and Portuguese phrases, were called "pidgin-english." The sound "pidgin" was supposed to be the Chinese attempt to pronounce the word "business." In the main, this hybrid speech was limited to a number of mispronounced English and Portuguese words, and for good measure a few Indian phrases, strung together according to Chinese idiom and construction. The words "mandarin" and "compradore" came from the Portuguese meaning to command and count, while "tiffin," "chit," "bazaar" and "coolie" were of Indian origin. Other duties of the linguists were to supply sampans for loading and unloading, and to attend to any business connected with the customs house in the city which the foreigners were not allowed to visit. Their fee was a hundred and twenty taels per vessel. Completing the circle of Chinese who came in contact with the foreigners were the servants and coolies who worked in the factories. It has been claimed they acted as spies whose duty it was to report to the authorities every action and, as much as they were able to understand, every conversation, which took place among foreigners.

When a ship arrived at Whampoa the Hoppo, accompanied by the co-hong, went out to inspect and measure her. It was the custom to give this official presents when he came on board, which Americans failed to do. When the Hoppo asked for his "sing-songs" he seemed displeased that none had been brought, but said he would overlook the matter since it was the *Empress of China's* first voyage to the Celestial Kingdom. He enjoined the officers, however, not to overlook the matter a second time. The tax was about four thousand dollars per vessel regardless of size and in addition each article was assessed, but the Chinese, whether buying or selling, paid the duty on goods. After a ship had been measured, the security merchant took out a permit for unloading and the linguist provided two sampans for carrying the cargo to Canton. Merchandise was discharged under the watchful eyes of mandarins hovering nearby in their boats. At

Canton everything was tabulated and when that was done the supercargoes were at liberty to sell, the choice of goods going to the co-hong, the residue to the small merchants from whom the linguist collected duty and settled with the ship's guarantor.

"Commerce here" wrote Major Shaw, "appears to be, and is, perhaps, as simple as any in the known world." Fourteen years later Captain Edmund Fanning stated, "The usages and customs of trade at Canton make it easy for the supercargoes to attend to their business there with dispatch; in fact, more so than at any other port of the world I have visited." Most of the foreign merchants seem to have agreed with this opinion, although there were some who felt that each nation should show an active protection of its citizens trading in China. On the whole, things went along smoothly enough as long as there was no government interference; between foreign and Chinese merchants relations were friendly, but the moment officials intervened business suffered and foreigners were compelled to submit to injustices. The Chinese held the whip hand—if anything displeased them they simply stopped trade, and, as this involved tremendous losses, a conciliatory attitude was essential to commerce.

Pwankeiqua offered Shaw and Randall a hundred and fifty dollars a picul* for their ginseng, a disappointingly low price compared to what it had brought the season before. A European friend advised them not to sell at once but to wait and exhaust the patience of the Chinese, a difficult thing to do as Randall remarked. Another member of the co-hong put the bid up to a hundred and fifty-five dollars which was accepted, although the price had later to be reduced because the bulk did not prove equal to the sample. Randall wrote to Alexander Hamilton that the ginseng had not been picked at the right season and was not properly culled and garbled to suit the Chinese taste. The remainder of the cargo was sold for about cost; the cordage and wine to the Europeans and the lead and iron, etc., to the Chinese.

The profits of the China trade, however, lay not in selling to the Chinese, but in buying teas for consumption abroad. As an English captain noted in his log, "At Whampoa you see English, French, Dutch, Danes, Swedes, Italians and Russians. The Americans, too, it seems, have overcome their distaste against

* A picul is the equivalent of about 132 pounds.

tea and have opened a trade for that commodity with the Chinese."

The quality of the tea was determined by the smallness of the leaves and the season in which it was picked. There were many different varieties and the Chinese were as particular about them as the Frenchman is about the vintage of his wines. Of black teas, the coarsest was Bohea, which was picked late in the season. A slightly better grade was Congou, exported in great quantities by the British East India Company. The two best grades of black tea were Souchang, scented with flowers, and Pekoe, composed of young spring buds. The mandarins used Pekoe packed in small cannisters to send as presents, but it was rarely exported, being, like certain wines, too delicate to travel. Of the five different kinds of green tea the cheapest was Twankay, which was frequently mixed with the better kinds for export. Hyson skin, or "Flourishing Spring," of which the best of the crop was picked early in the season and prepared with great care, was popular for export. The choicest of green teas were Gunpowder, or Pearl tea, and Yu Tsien, meaning "before the rains"; both were picked in the first warmth of spring.

All tea leaves were carefully dried and rolled by hand, the black trampled on to make them pack more closely, while the delicate green leaves were shaken in baskets before sealing them in chests. When the market in Canton was cleared and business over for the season, contracts were made for the next year, sometimes at fixed prices and sometimes at opening prices. These contracts rain into hundreds of thousands of dollars but no written agreement was ever drawn up, nor was anything sealed or attested. A wilful breach of contract was never known to occur. In fact, so proverbial was the honesty of the co-hong that there was no such thing as a receipt or a check book and large amounts of money were carried to and fro by the compradores.

The first Americans at Canton traded under certain disadvantages. They were on their own without government backing and with no powerful organization behind them such as the British had in their East India Company, which afforded those trading under its aegis a unified front. The Danes, Imperialists, Swedes and Dutch also had regular establishments, and the French maintained a permanent consul, although he was not recognized as a government official by the Chinese. The Americans were far from home and without ports of refuge such as the European settlements of Macao, Manila, Malacca,

Batavia, Sumatra and the Indian ports. On the other hand, their very inexperience was an asset, for they could not be accused of intriguing against the Celestial Empire, nor had they any past history such as the Portuguese of lawless depradations, or the British of armed defense. The Europeans were compelled to pay for their cargoes in specie but Americans procured teas in exchange for the produce of their own country.

A very important factor in the American trade was the superiority of the crews which were composed of young men of good stock, either from New England farms or seafaring families and of a much higher class than the European sailors, who for the most part were riffraff enlisted or shanghaied out of the gutters. The American youth went to sea, generally when he was still in his teens, because he wanted to, because it was a glorious adventure, and because there was a chance of good remuneration for his work. Members of the crews were allowed to buy shipping space and were therefore vitally interested in the outcome of the voyage. They worked willingly and hard but they still had time for a little amusement, as the following account shows:

"The sailors had what they called sailors' comfort every Saturday afternoon in the middle watch. It consisted in overhauling their chests and bags, or mending their clothes—on the system, as they said, of putting a patch next to a patch as being neighborly, but never a patch upon a patch as that was beggarly. . . . No happier crew ever rocked the cradle of the deep than the one of which the *Citizen* was composed. This was the result of uniformly taut but considerate treatment, the best of food, good grog, and no needless botheration, while the utmost harmony prevailed between the captain and his officers."

Major Samuel Shaw wrote that after bargaining with a Chinese for several days the following conversation took place:

"You are not Englishman?"

"No."

"But you speak English word and when you first come I can no tell difference; but now I understand very well. When I speak Englishman his price, he say 'So much—take it,—let alone.' I tell him, 'No, my friend, I give you so much.' He look at me— 'Go to hell, you damned rascal; what! you come here—set a price my goods?' Truly, Massa Taipan, I see very well you no hap Englishman. All Chinaman love very much your country."

Major Shaw added, "Thus far it may be supposed the fellow's remarks pleased me. Justice obliges me to add his conclusion: 'All men come China first time very good gentlemen, all same you. But I think two three more time you come Canton you make all same Englishman too.'"

Europeans and Americans alike were forced to submit to Chinese customs and to yield to the ancient dynastic usage of the Chinese in regard to their treatment of outer barbarians. All foreigners were held in contempt because of their complete ignorance of either the written or spoken language, although according to the laws of the Empire no Chinese was allowed to teach his language to an outsider. The conduct of European sailors was often a cause of disturbance and the French and British seamen carried their hatred to such an extent that they were constantly quarreling, until finally the Chinese allocated the former on an island which afterwards bore the name of French Island. To the peace-loving Chinese such conduct was incomprehensible, and when the quarrels assumed serious proportions trade was stopped and all nations suffered.

The *Empress of China* sailed from Whampoa on December 28th, 1784, with all hands on board except Thomas Randall, who remained in Canton in the interests of Major Shaw and himself. When Major Shaw arrived in New York on May 10th, 1785, he discovered that Daniel Parker had gone to Europe, bankrupt, so the accounts were settled with Thomas Fitzsimmons and Gouverneur Morris, attorney for Robert Morris. After the settlement was made there was a profit of over thirty thousand dollars, more than twenty-five per cent of the original capital employed.

5

THE ROLE OF MACAO; THE OPIUM TRADE

The account of the *Empress of China's* reception in Canton might well apply to any American ship in the East India trade up to 1840, for there were few changes in commercial relations until after the Opium War (1840-42). When Samuel Shaw returned home, he wrote a report to the Secretary of the Department of Foreign Affairs, John Jay, who laid the letter before Congress. This august body instructed the Secretary to inform Shaw, "that Congress feel a peculiar satisfaction in the successful issue of this first effort of American citizens to establish a direct trade with China, which does much honor to its undertakers and conductors."

Shortly after the *Empress of China* returned home, the *Pallas* put into New York from Canton with Thomas Randall on board. She carried fifty thousand dollars' worth of teas, which had been taken on the joint account of Shaw and Randall and which were sold to Robert Morris. The Philadelphia merchant foresaw so much profit in the China trade that he wished to re-engage the two partners to act in his behalf on an extensive plan which would have meant their remaining in Canton for several years, but as terms could not be agreed upon, the matter was dropped. The two ships between them carried nearly a million pounds of tea from China to America.

Under the patronage of his old friend General Knox, Shaw accepted the appointment of first secretary in the war office, but soon resigned the position to enter once more in the pursuit of commerce. Engaged by Isaac Sears and other New York merchants, he and Randall—without whom he refused to go—embarked again for the Orient, this time on the ship *Hope*, James Magee, captain. Congress commissioned Major Shaw consul at Canton and Thomas Randall vice-consul, although neither of them received a salary or perquisites. The appointments were titles, in recognition of former services, rather than offices to give protection to American citizens abroad; as yet, the government displayed no positive attitude toward the East India trade, and though it was recognized as a valuable asset to the growing nation, it was carried on under the responsibility of individuals.

In the season of 1786-87, there were five American ships at Canton: the *Experiment*, the *Empress of China* and the *Hope*, all from New York, the *Canton* from Philadelphia, and the *Grand Turk*, belonging to Elias Hasket Derby of Salem. The *Grand Turk*, Captain Ebenezer West, arrived in China just after the *Hope* and was the first Massachusetts vessel to sail Far Eastern waters. Her voyages were so profitable they were an inspiration to every New England ship owner.

In the same season there was a great increase in British shipping, both in tonnage and number of ships and, as might be expected, the price of teas advanced twenty-five per cent. The French were doing little business; a new company had been formed, but they themselves declared, *qu'elle ne durera pas longtemps*. Spain was interested more in Manila than Canton, Holland in Batavia, and Portugal in Macao, so the rivalry lay between the British and the Americans. The Americans were welcomed cordially by both Chinese and continentals, but the British exhibited a marked change of manner. The directors of the British East India Company had ordered their supercargoes neither to assist nor in any way encourage American trade, and although formal calls were exchanged no further attentions were shown. It was generally felt that the English were aiming not only at the monopoly of the European tea trade, but at exclusive commerce in the Far East. New business houses were being constructed in India and the government prohibited subjects living in that country to sell ships to foreigners.

Major Shaw, having decided to stay in China while Thomas Randall returned to America, left for Macao in company with other merchants at the end of the season. The Chinese, afraid lest the Europeans obtain a foothold in the Celestial Empire, refused to allow them to remain in Canton through the year, so, in the spring, at the close of the northeast monsoon, after the ships had left with their home-bound cargoes, the foreigners repaired to the Portuguese city on the island of Hsiang Shan, eighty-eight miles down river, where they remained for the summer. The annual departure from Canton was quite an affair and required fifteen or twenty boats for each factory to carry passengers, compradores' men, cooks, servants and boats' crews, not to mention supplies for the trip (it took three or four days) of food and wine. When a pass for Macao was desired, the linguist was sent for. It was his duty to apply to the co-hong, who sent a respectful petition to the Hoppo that the request might be granted. The Hoppo then issued passports which had to be countersigned at West Fort and Che-Nae, and certified lists of articles required for the trip, both personal and those that were to be sold in Macao.

The city, enclosed within a wall, was built in amphitheater shape and sloped gently from the hills toward a magnificent promenade, the Praya Grande, running along the east sea wall. The scene was picturesque and pleasantly European after the long months of Chinese architecture, and it was bracing to inhale the fresh sea breezes instead of the fetid odors of the Pearl River. A different diet, too—fish, poultry, pork and an abundance of fresh vegetables—was a welcome change. Aside from the beneficial effects of climate and diet, it was a relaxation to escape for a while the rigorous restrictions under which foreigners labored at Canton.

From the time the Portuguese first leased Macao from the Emperor for five hundred taels a year it steadily grew in importance until it became the great trading center between China and the West. It was especially prosperous during the first half of the eighteenth century, but its ascendancy waned with the cession of Hong Kong to the British after the Opium War and from then on its trade declined. The idea that Macao was settled through conquest is erroneous: its possession by the Portuguese may be ascribed rather to Imperial bounty and the ground rent was paid regularly until 1849, when the Governor declared Macao a free port and ordered the Chinese customs house closed. That the Portuguese considered themselves tenants and not conquerors is shown in the following letter written by order of the Senate to the Emperor K'ang Hsi in 1719:

The Portuguese of Macao who govern the place, Manoel Vincente Rosa, &c. with all the others, have always received immense favors of your Imperial Majesty, whose name fills all the world, and lately a new one bestowed upon us by not being included in the prohibition of navigating the southern seas; we have more than ten thousand mouths to provide for. The favor of not being comprehended in the prohibition is above all comparison great, and certainly we can never acknowledge it as we ought. To show in some way our thankfulness, we have selected a few articles, which we at present transmit to the Viceroy, begging him to have the goodness to present them to your Imperial Majesty, and we shall be very happy, &c. Macao, March 1, 1719.

(Signed) M. J. Rosa, &c.

Among other presents sent to the Emperor were several cases of the "very best European wine," Amostrina snuff, perfume, gold lace and fire-locks.

By the end of the eighteenth century, the inhabitants of the island were far from being purebread Europeans. In the two hundred and seventy years the Portuguese had been in China, they had intermarried with Indians, Malays, and other Oriental races to such an extent they no longer retained their native physiognomy and few of them had been west of the Cape of Good Hope. Their language, though called Portuguese, was so mixed with eastern dialects as to be unintelligible to newly arrived Europeans from Lisbon. The descendants of these mixed marriages were known as "mesticos" or Indian-Portuguese.

The government of the island came under two headings: the Chinese population, more numerous than the European, had their own separate government at the head of which were mandarins appointed by the Emperor, and under them Chinese customs officials. All foreigners were subject to Portuguese administration, the authority vested in a governor and a senate, a syndic or civil judge, and a vicar-general for ecclesiastical affairs. The salary of the governor was twelve hundred taels a year, a sum quite insufficient to support his position and which he was forced to augment by taking an active interest in the trade of the island. Opium was contraband in China proper and could not legally be admitted into any Chinese port, but this ruling did not extend to Macao and the officials had an interest in all shipments smuggled from the island to the mainland, although in 1720 King John had proclaimed that, "the Governor is allowed to trade neither in his own name nor in that of any other person."

View of the Praya Grande, Macao, c. 1855, attributed to Youqua (active 1840-70). In this view, Chinese and Western vessels are seen against a background of Macao's handsome forts, churches and public buildings. (Peabody Museum of Salem, gift of Mrs. Beverly R. Robinson; photograph by Mark Sexton.)

View of Victoria, Hong Kong, c. 1855, attributed to Youqua. In this painting, one of a set of four large and highly important port views, British vessels are predominant among foreign shipping. (Peabody Museum of Salem, gift of Mrs. Beverly R. Robinson; photograph by Mark Sexton.)

"It is said," wrote Major Shaw, "that in the season of 1784-85 his emoluments from this article did not fall short of forty thousand dollars, which is not to be wondered at when it is considered that upwards of two thousand chests valued on an average of three hundred and fifty dollars each are annually brought to China."

Opium was first mentioned in Chinese literature in the eighth century when it was described as a medicine for troubles of the bowels. It could not have been used extensively, however, until the eighteenth century as there is no mention of it in the writings of the Catholic missionaries, who, so meticulous in reporting all details of Chinese life, would surely have referred to it had there been any prevalent use of the drug. The Chinese have many names for it: great smoke, black earth, black commodity, and *foreign medicine*. It is probable that the Dutch introduced opium into China from Java, where it was often mixed with tobacco. It was also imported, though not in large quantities, by the Portuguese. In the eighteenth century the trade mounted to such proportions that the Emperor Yung Cheng issued an edict against smoking it, and toward the end of the century a restriction was placed on importation and it was banned throughout the empire. In 1820 His Excellency the Viceroy of Canton warned customs officials not to allow any ship carrying opium to be admitted into the port, cautioning them "not to view this document as a mere matter of form and so tread within the net of the law, for you will find your escape as impracticable as it is for a man to bite his own navel."

During the latter half of the eighteenth and the early half of the nineteenth centuries there was little pretense on the part of either the Chinese or the foreigners to respect opium regulations. Illegal duties were levied by petty officials, foreigners continued to import the drug, and both found it profitable. Opium was smuggled mostly in British bottoms because of the large accessible supply in India, but American ships were by no means guiltless of offense. It was a common proceeding for Americans to add a cargo of Turkish opium on their way east; the drug was the foundation of many an American fortune as well as British. Only one American firm in Canton, Olyphant and Co., refused to have anything to do with the trade. Indian opium was prepared with great care to suit the Chinese taste, as well it might be since the export tax brought in a tremendous revenue. It was stated in one of the many parliamentary debates about the shipping of opium that, financially, it was a matter of life and death to the British government in India.

In 1787 the Governor of Macao found his "emoluments" considerably reduced because the English, instead of transferring opium to Portuguese vessels, ordered one of their own ships to Lintin in the Pearl River to act as a depository for the drug. Chinese merchants repaired to this receiving ship, paid in advance for goods, and for every chest received handed over twenty dollars cumshaw to the petty officers who were plying to and fro in their sampans watching the proceedings with eagle eye.

The Portuguese were the only foreigners allowed to own property on the island and other Europeans, when renting houses, were compelled to submit to any unjust claim of the owners. Residences might be let in wretched condition but if improved at the expense of the lessee, higher rents were demanded by the proprietors, who, if the demands were not met, took over the houses at the end of the season when the tenants returned to Canton, no matter for how many years the places had been leased. On one occasion the Swedish house, the best in Macao, which had cost the company eight thousand dollars to repair and improve, was unwillingly relinquished to the Governor whose lady had taken a fancy to it, and the Swedes were compelled to move into His Excellency's house—much to their disadvantage. Another time a British supercargo was ordered to vacate the premises he had rented and put in living order so that they might be turned over to a new syndic who was expected shortly from Goa. This he refused to do and barricaded his doors. The next day his house was broken into and he was seized and held in the dungeon of the tronco for almost a week. The syndic, happily a little more punctilious than his countrymen, refused to live in the house when he heard of the man's plight—that is, longer than it would take him to find another.

Except for the Governor and his wife and one or two of the leading families, foreign merchants saw little of the Portuguese, whom they considered idle, consequently poor, and ignorant and superstitious in extreme. Two and a half centuries of indolent living had obliterated all traces of the vigor and initiative which characterized the early settlers on the island. In spite of the many differences existing between natives and visitors, the merchants were far more comfortable at Macao than in the factories. Faro and dancing were the chief amusements, boating was another pastime, and parties were frequently formed to attend the public concerts which were held twice a week. Macao at that time had the reputation of being the most immoral place in the world, a kind of Monte Carlo of the Pacific, and was filled with gambling halls and other places of pleasure where the gallants, when not enjoying balls and dinners with the ladies, might betake themselves.

As for the sailors, Macao was a port beyond compare, offering every amusement to those who had endured long months at sea. Chinese orders were stringent in insisting that foreigners must not have any connection whatsoever with Chinese women, the penalty being either imprisonment or a heavy fine, and while the crews at Whampoa no doubt managed to evade this proclamation, nevertheless Macao offered more freedom with less danger of running afoul of the law.

Notorious as was the reputation of the city, it presented a saintly front clustered with churches, monasteries and convents which, as well as judicial and executive buildings, hospitals and jails, were handsomely constructed of shining white stone. Of private houses the most famous was "Casa de Horta," built on rising ground overlooking the city and harbor, and with a garden celebrated not only for its beauty, but as being the spot where the Portuguese poet Luiz de Camöens wrote the "Lusiad," immortalizing his adventurous countrymen who first doubled the Cape of Good Hope. The houses were either painted white or washed with lime, and with the public buildings formed a city glistening in the sunshine and reflected in the blue waters below.

There were never at any time many foreign women in Macao; a few Portuguese, some wives of ship's captains, a handful of colonial Dutch women from Java and one or two wives of missionaries. Her Excellency the Governor's wife was "sensible, artful, and when she pleases, very agreeable." It was a custom to entertain their Excellencies at least once, and sometimes more often, at dinner although they never felt it their duty to return the courtesy. The Governor, a native of Goa, was singularly uninformed for one in his position and from all accounts must have been rather dull. At a dinner in the year 1787 he asked whether or not the war between England and the American colonies was yet at an end! A senator, on overhearing the question and on being informed that England had lost much in losing the colonies, replied, "Ah, but they have taken Pulo Pinang."

Whether or not the conduct of the Portuguese was advantageous to other Europeans following in their footsteps, their tenure of Macao was of undoubted benefit. The island was a haven for all foreigners; in the heat of the summer, in times of sickness, in avoiding the ire of the Cantonese officials, and it was a base for missionary activity. Though nominally under Chinese sovereignty, it was a meeting ground of the West and the only one off the coast of China where foreigners might be free from the ever constant surveillance of petty officialdom.

6

SAMUEL SHAW AND THE *MASSACHUSETTS*

Major Shaw returned home in 1790 for the launching of his ship, the *Massachusetts*, nine hundred tons. She was built in Quincy especially for the China trade on Shaw's orders for the firm of Shaw and Randall by contract with Eli Hayden of Braintree and the master builder was Daniel Briggs, of a family famed for its shipbuilders. When brought to Boston under jury masts, the *Massachusetts* excited considerable attention for she was the largest merchant ship at that time in America. Numerous applications were made for stations on board and curious throngs swarmed over her decks, among them French and British officers from men-of-war in the harbor, who were unanimous in their admiration. In spite of compliments and praise, the crew was changed three times before sailing because of a last minute prediction by old Moll Pitcher of Lynn that the vessel would be lost with all hands. The *Massachusetts* sailed from Boston on March 28th, 1790, Job Prince, captain, and the first and second officers were Josiah Roberts and Amasa Delano. Also on board were the owner and his brother Nathaniel. As the ship neared Java Head it was discovered the reckoning was out and the vessel off her course. "All this loss of time," wrote Amasa Delano, "happened on account of our not having any chronometer on board, nor any officer who knew anything about lunar observations. Every officer should furnish himself with a good brass sextant. A wooden sextant is worse than nothing." The

Massachusetts was not alone in lacking proper instruments—the wonder is that American ships got to Canton at all!

In Java friendly natives brought fowl, parrots, monkeys, pigs, plantains, melons, sweet potatoes, coconuts, oranges, green turtles, and a great number of malacca canes to exchange with the crew in return for old knives, old clothes or other trifles, but should a Dutch boat appear on the horizon they beat a hasty retreat, being in great fear of the Hollanders. This, perhaps, gives a little insight into Dutch methods of colonization at that time.

In Batavia, because of Major Shaw's rank of consul at Canton and because the *Massachusetts* was a credit to them everywhere, the Americans were courteously received by the officials of the island though the Governor was suprised, indeed somewhat shocked, to find a consul doing business like an ordinary speculating merchant. He remarked that if the American government were unable to pay its officers it would do a better job to keep them at home. Major Shaw had expected to change his cargo at Batavia for one suitable to Canton but the Dutch authorities refused a permit.

Just off the China coast the ship was caught in a typhoon but weathered the gale despite Moll Pitcher's warning, although a Dutch ship was lost with four hundred thousand dollars on board and a Danish ship was completely dismasted. In Canton, the *Massachusetts* was visited constantly by all the Europeans, who examined her from stern to bow and acknowledged her to be the handsomest vessel in port. She was loaded mainly with green timber which had been taken on board while it was still wet, and the lower hold thus filled had been tightly closed from Boston to China. When it was opened the air was found to be so corrupt that it put out a lighted candle, the beef was almost boiled, the hoops rotted and were falling off and the inside covered with a thick blue mold more than half an inch thick. At the time a mistaken idea prevailed that air should be prevented from circulating through the hold, yet not many years later Americans had learned how to transport ice from Labrador which they sold from Calcutta to Canton!

Since the cargo of the *Massachusetts* was practically ruined and the firm's debts had increased, Major Shaw decided to sell the ship to the Danish company who were anxious to replace theirs, which had been dismasted in the typhoon. John Bartlett, a member of the crew, reported in his log that the vessel was sold for $65,000 and "if such were the truth," says Tyler Dennett, "the venture had by no means ended in disaster, for it is unlikely that the *Massachusetts* cost more than $40,000." The crew, thirty-eight Americans and twenty-three Englishmen, were obliged to find other ships on which to sail. John Bartlett and eight other men shipped on the *Gustavus* bound for the northwest coast of America. Amasa Delano, having earned a great reputation repairing the Danish ship, had no trouble in finding a place on board a British vessel, where, he wrote, although he was an American with all the associations of the late war, the officers treated him with courtesy. With American independence of manner he insisted in being under orders to the captain only.

By the turn of the century American trade with the Orient was well established. American ships sailed the seven seas, always with one aim, to find something they could exhange in Canton for teas. Yankee mariners fought with pirates in the Mediterranean and off the Malay coast, they rounded South America in search for furs and added sandalwood and bêche-de-mer to their cargoes in the Pacific islands, they carried ice from Labrador to India and picked up coffee and spices on their way home. The government was still in no position to render active help or protection, but trade, though heterogeneous and lacking cohesion, thrived from the beginning under the impetus of the youths—they were on average less than thirty years of age—who engaged in it.

The sea brought to Americans new freedom of thought, a new confidence in themselves. Captains begged for American crews, pointing out their superiority over all other nationalities, and everybody shared in this enthusiasm. The China trade was the source of wealth in the northern states before the era of mills and factories, but more than that it was the stimulant which awakened the imagination of the people and added color and adventure to their lives. Youths and old men thrilled to stories of savage Indians, of Hawaii chiefs draped in capes of multi-colored plumage, of Tripolitan pirates and of unfathomable Chinese merchants, which, in the telling lost no flavor. Tea, of course, was the great incentive but almost as important, there was not a woman in America who did not crave a brilliant Chinese shawl, a piece of carved ivory or a set of Canton plates.

7

THE FUR TRADE

On his second voyage to Canton Major Shaw noted in his *Journal* that it must be "a most satisfactory consideration to every American that his country can carry on its commerce with China under advantages, if not in many respects superior, yet in all cases equal, to those possessed by any other people." He was, of course, referring to the fact that Americans obtained their teas in return for ginseng while the Europeans purchased principally with specie, but the value of the drug had been optimistically overestimated and something else had to be found—something the Chinese would accept in return for teas.

Captain Cook's voyage to the northwest coast of America proved to the English that a lucrative fur trade might be carried on with the Indians and several British ships were sent from Canton to collect pelts. Ledyard's reports eventually spurred Americans to the same purpose.

About the time of John Ledyard's death a ship was sent out of Boston. It was the *Columbia*, two hundred and thirteen tons, built by the famous Briggs brothers and financed by Joseph Barrell, Samuel Brown, Captain Hatch, Charles Bulfinch, the architect, J. M. Pintard and John Derby. The command was given to Captain John Kendrick and second in command was John Gray, former officer of the Continental navy, captain of the ninety-ton sloop *Lady Washington*, which accompanied the *Columbia*. The two vessels ran into storms off Cape Horn and so arrived at Nootka Sound too late in the season to do any trading. They were forced to lay over until the next year by which time their provisions were running low and Captain Kendrick ordered Captain Gray to proceed to Canton with what furs had been collected.

When Gray arrived in China he asked Thomas Randall to undertake the sale of the fifteen hundred otter skins he had brought with him. It was unfortunate for the two Americans that the skins were so fine, because the Viceroy took a fancy to them and that, under the Chinese system, could mean only one thing—the co-hong would be obliged to purchase them and present them to his Excellency. The bidding was therefore low but as the *Columbia* was bound to sail in season there was nothing to do except agree to the terms.

Randall wrote to Alexander Hamilton concerning the fur trade; he stated the demand was great but the Americans were unable to profit from their advantages because of separate interests and lack of any established communal factory. He added that could vessels carrying a cargo of sea otter, the most valuable fur, stay over a season, they would get good prices, but transients were open to imposition. The profits in American trade, however, lay in quick barter; it was carried out on no such scale as the British trade, nor could Americans afford to lay over a season, especially since they had no organization like the East India Company behind them. Randall was correct in his estimate as far as it went, but he failed to take into consideration the tenacity of the Yankee trader, who, once he found something that was in demand in the China market, was going to get it there in spite of any obstacle.

Massachusetts was quick to see the advantages of the northwest fur trade. Although the *Columbia's* first voyage was not financially successful—she arrived home with a damaged cargo and on top of that found the price of tea was depressed because fourteen vessels had already made port that season—she was promptly refitted for a second voyage. On her initial venture the *Columbia* was the first American ship to circumnavigate the globe; on her next, her commander, Captain Gray, discovered the mouth of the Columbia River, an even more important achievement because of the great weight it gave to American claims to the northwest coast.

John Boit, the sixteen-year-old mate of the *Columbia*, logged for May 12th, 1792, "This day saw an appearance of a spacious harbor abreast the ship, haul'd our wind for it, observed two sandbars making off, with passage between them to a fine river... The river extended to the N.E. as far as the eye could reach and water fit to drink as far down as the Bars at the entrance. We directed our course up this noble River in search of a Village. The beach was lined with natives who ran along shore following the Ship. Soon after, above twenty canoes came off, and brought a good lot of Furs and Salmon, which last they sold two for a board nail. The furs we likewise bought cheap for copper and cloth. They appeared to view the Ship with great astonishment."

"May 18. Captain Gray named this river *Columbia*."

Captain Gray commanded the *Columbia* on her two famous voyages, but great credit is also due to Captain Kendrick of whom a contemporary enthusiastically wrote, "He was the first American to burst forth into the world and traverse those distant regions which were then but little known. He taught many of his countrymen the way to wealth and the method of navigating distant seas with ease and safety." Captain Kendrick ranged the seas for the United States much as Cook had circled the globe for England. The northwest coast so fascinated him, perhaps because he had the vision to foresee its potentialities, that he bought large tracts of lands from the Indians, but he did not confine his explorations to the rugged shores of North America. He sailed as well among the islands of the Pacific and found sandalwood growing wild on the Sandwich Islands. This fragrant wood was used by the Chinese to make joss sticks to burn in their temples as offerings to the gods. Captain Kendrick was accidentally killed in Hawaii in 1794 by salutes from a ship's guns, one of which, through an oversight, was loaded with grapeshot.

The *Columbia* and the *Lady Washington* sailed from Boston, and for years Boston had such a monopoly in the fur trade that all Americans were known to the Indians as "Boston-men." The trade was in full swing by 1792 and proved a tremendous asset to a people poor in specie, but rich in ships and crews. In return for pelts, teas, the Golden Fleece of the China trade, were carried in American bottoms not only home but to Europe as well. Americans obtained furs from the Indians for almost nothing— beads and mirrors and when these became too common, cloth, iron and nails—but it was a hazardous undertaking. Navigating Cape Horn where a ship might run into floating icebergs or be washed by tempestuous waves required skill and nerve and there was not a seaman who failed to give a sigh of relief once his ship was headed north into the blue waters of the Pacific. Then the Indians were treacherous to deal with; it is true thay had not always been fairly treated by the white men but they never failed to retaliate for any insult, either real or fancied, in the most barbarous fashion. Captain Kendrick's son was killed and so was a mate of the *Columbia*.

In 1803, the *Boston* arrived on the coast and the Captain presented a fowling gun as a token of friendship to the chief with whom he was trading. The next day the brave chief returned the gun broken and remarked it was no good. This was too great a strain on the Captain's self-control and he promptly called the man a liar. Within twenty-four hours the Indians surrounded and seized the ship and massacred everyone on board with the exception of two of the crew who were taken into slavery. One of them, John Jewitt, an armorer, was forced to make weapons. After three years' imprisonment, the captives effected their escape on the brig *Lydia*.

As the fur trade grew men not only sailed around the coast but also a frenzied race overland began. In the beginning of the nineteenth century John Jacob Astor formed a company to colonize Indian territory and thus monopolize the trade. In 1811 he sent out the ill-fated *Tonquin* with a company of merchants on board, who, together with a band of voyagers from Canada, were to found Astoria. Things went along smoothly enough for the first few months, but from misunderstandings grew a bitter hatred between the Indians and the white men. One day the Indians treacherously seized the *Tonquin* and when it was obvious there was no chance of escape a member of the crew ignited a powder keg and like Samson destroyed his enemies together with himself. Astoria was sold to the British in 1812.

The search for furs led not only to the northwest coast but to all the islands of the Pacific. The *Betsy* of New York, ninety-three tons, under Captain Edmund Fanning with a crew of twenty-seven men, most of them from New England, reached Más Afuera, one of the Juan Fernández Islands off the coast of Chile, in 1798 and loaded with seal skins. Fanning's *Voyages and Discoveries in the South Seas, 1792-1832*, is informative in describing the adventurous courage that led American sailors to navigate every body of water, known or unknown, in the world. The captain sailed for twenty-five years, was agent for seventy expeditions and it was his petition that led Congress to authorize an exploring expedition under Commodore Wilkes. He discovered Fanning's Island, lying twelve hundred miles south of Honolulu.

From Más Afuera the *Betsy* sailed to the Marquesas, the Washington and Ladrone Islands. At the last named place, Captain Fanning picked up survivors, among them three women, of an East India Company ship. When they arrived at Macao, the mandarin at first refused to issue a chop because of the women on board but the matter was finally settled when the chief of the Company promised to send them away on the first available vessel. The *Betsy* was then allowed to leave for Canton, where the cargo of furs was sold and another of teas, silks, and chinaware taken on board. South of Sumatra on her homeward voyage she was surprised by twenty-nine Malay piratical proas but managed to put them to rout. "Our ship," wrote the Captain, "showed fourteen guns; four, however, false, but so painted as exactly to resemble our iron ones."

The *Betsy* returned home after an absence of twenty-three months. The net profits of this voyage were $52,300 for the owners and the amount paid into the national treasury as duties three times more than the cost of the ship. She was the first American vessel entirely manned by native Americans—all of them, incidentally, under twenty-eight—to sail around the world from New York.

The *Betsy* was by no means the only, or even the first, small ship to be sent on such a voyage; indeed, it was the rule rather than the exception that American ships in the Canton-northwest trade were small. Undaunted by the fact they were too poor to build larger and more suitable craft, the merchants nevertheless persevered and existing logs give thrilling testimony to the courage of those who sailed these tiny vessels. In 1790, the seventy-ton brigantine *Hope* was sent out from Boston to the northwest coast under Joseph Ingraham, former mate to Captain Gray, and met the ninety-ton *Lady Washington* in Canton. Captain Kendrick had been nearly four years away from home! It was on this voyage that Captain Ingraham discovered and named the Washington group of the Marquesas.

The long journey from east to west coast was broken by visits to the Falkland Islands, Juan Fernandez, or, more appealing still to the sailors, the Sandwich Islands. Then came a long season of trading with the Indians, perhaps as much as a year and a half on the northwest coast, then back again to the Sandwich Islands where any of the crew suffering from scurvy might recover with fresh fruits and sunshine.

Hawaii seems to have been the favorite port of call—the natives were as gay as the Indians were saturnine and were even more than hospitable, allowing their women to consort freely with strangers. It was not uncommon for a vessel to be crowded with island mermaids who thought nothing of swimming out two or three miles from shore for a visit; sometimes there were so many that numbers of them had to swim back again! The Sandwich Islanders were soft spoken and gentle in their manner and alluring with their delicate features and small, graceful hands. By way of adornment, they wore wreaths of flowers or bracelets and necklaces of shells. On ceremonial occasions the men attired themselves picturesquely in capes made entirely of yellow feathers.

In 1790, a romantic character, John Young, a seaman, arrived in Hawaii and remained to marry a native. He became King Kamehameha's advisor and through him traders bargained for sandalwood to complete their cargoes. One of his sons served with distinction in the navy during the War of 1812.

The Fijis were more treacherous but New Englanders, as undeterred by an occasional cannibalistic feast as they were by scalping, continued to visit the islands to gather edible birds' nests and bêche-de-mer for the delectation of mandarins.

At Timor, Amasa Delano found a manuscript history of the *Pandora*, the vessel sent out in search of the mutineers of the *Bounty*. The first person to visit the now famous Pitcairn Island where the mutineers and their Tahitian wives had settled was Captain Mayhew Folger, on the *Topaz*, in search of furs. The only survivor of the mutiny was Alexander Smith, living in patriarchal manner as mentor to the thirty-four women and children who survived their husbands and fathers. The story of Captain Folger's amazement is well known. On his arrival at the island, the natives who boarded his ship not only greeted him in English but insisted on saying grace before each meal!

On another voyage, Amasa Delano picked up eight stranded Japanese in one of the Pacific Islands and took them to Canton where, much to the surprise of everyone, it was discovered that, although they were not Chinese, they could understand the written characters. With the aid of a Chinese servant, Delano learned they came from "Osaka in the island of Nippon." The eight men were returned to their native land through the intervention of the Dutch, the only foreigners allowed the privilege of trade in Japan, since the islanders, resentful of the conduct of the Portuguese, had created a barrier against the Europeans in the seventeenth century.

Sea otter, so admired by the mandarins, brought the best prices in Canton, but the Yankees also went after the sealskins. Seals were found on the islands off South America—the Falklands, Más Afuera, St. Paul and Amsterdam, as well as off the coast of California. The luckless creatures were killed by clubbing them over the head and groups of sealers often remained on the islands to catch the animals and cure the skins while their ships traded up and down the coast, or until the arrival of other company ships to pick them up. It was a lucrative trade while it lasted, but as mothers, fathers and babies were clubbed indiscriminately, the supply could not last forever and the seal became practically extinct. The pelts brought only a few dollars in Canton, but because seals were so easy to catch, cargoes were often made up of as many as a thousand skins.

8

THE HEIGHT OF SALEM'S GLORY: THE SPICE TRADE, BOWDITCH, DERBY, PEABODY

While the men of Boston were busily engaged collecting the pelts, the mariners of Salem were founding fortunes in the pepper trade. The first to discover pepper growing wild near Benkulen on the southwest coast of Sumatra was Captain Jonathan Carnes, who hurried home to report his find. He was immediately sent out on the fast schooner, the *Rajah*, one hundred and thirty tons, and his destination kept secret. When he returned with a shipload of pungent spice, the owners realized a profit of seven hundred per cent! Such a secret could not be held long, however (although Carnes did manage to make three voyages before the news leaked out), and soon Salem ships were navigating the then uncharted, dangerous coral reefs as easily as they sailed the coast of New England and the name of Salem was synonymous with daring and enterprise. Her ships bartered at Batavia and Java for sugar and rice, at Manila for hemp and indigo, at Mocha for coffee, at the Spice Islands for cinnamon and clove and nutmeg, at Zanzibar for gum-copal, and Madeira for wine.

The hazards of navigation were not the only perils Salem men encountered; those they were able to master, but they could not always defend themselves against sudden, ruthless native attacks and many a young man was buried on the other side of the world with a kris in his ribs. In 1831 the natives of Kuala Batu captured the *Friendship*, killed the first mate and wounded several seamen. Captain Endicott, who was ashore at the time of the capture, but who saw what had happened, hastily made for Muckie in a small boat to enlist the aid of three American vessels there. The *Friendship* was recaptured, set sail and returned to Salem. A year later the United States frigate *Potomac* bombarded Kuala Batu as punishment.

At the height of Salem's glory, one of her sons added further to her prestige: in 1802 Nathaniel Bowditch published *The New American Practical Navigator,* a work that made American ships the fastest ever to sail. It was a book that no one could overlook, not even the British who were prone to disregard American publications, and there was not an American sailor who did not profit from its instructions. Amasa Delano, sailing on the *Massachusetts,* had complained about loss of time because the reckoning was out. The *Practical Navigator* saved time, but more important, added considerably to the safety of human lives at sea. Bowditch knew his astronomy so well that on a homeward voyage he sailed straight into Salem harbor and docked his ship without a mishap while a snowstorm raged and not a landmark was in sight!

Of Salem's merchant princes, the most eminent was Elias Hasket Derby, whose fleet was known the world over (*see frontispiece portrait*). He was the second son of Richard Derby, an ardent patriot who gave money, guns and ships to the Continental government, and his brother John took the first news of Concord and Lexington to England and eight years later brought back the word that peace had been declared. Elias started his career at an early age in his father's counting rooms. In 1784 he sent one of his ships, the *Grand Turk,* Captain Ingersoll in command, to the Cape of Good Hope to exchange rum, cheese, salt and butter for Bohea tea, but Captain Ingersoll was not able to buy the tea because ships bound for Europe were forbidden to break bulk at the Cape. In order to make up his cargo he sailed for the coast of Guinea to pick up ivory and gold dust, but would not consider taking on board a single slave. Derby, he told Samuel Shaw, who was homeward bound from Canton, would rather sink the whole capital employed than directly or indirectly be concerned in so infamous a traffic. A year later, the *Grand Turk* appeared in Canton and Derby's ships were the first to be seen from the United States in Bombay, Siam and Mocha.

The *Grand Turk* was the first New England vessel to compete in the China trade. When she appeared off Naugus Head

Nathaniel Bowditch (1773-1838), oil portrait by Charles Osgood, commissioned by the East India Marine Society, 1835. Bowditch is portrayed, at age 62, working below a bust of the Marquis de la Place, the French astronomer whose four-volume work, La Mécanique Céleste, *he earned global renown by translating. Over a nine-year period, Bowditch made five sea voyages, rising from ship's clerk to master, supercargo, and part-owner of his last vessel. In 1802, he published* The New American Practical Navigator, *a revision of John Hamilton Moore's handbook of navigation, with some 8,000 corrections, a work still in use today. (Peabody Museum of Salem, gift of the East India Marine Society; photograph by Mark Sexton.)*

Joseph Peabody (1757-1844), posthumous oil portrait by Charles Osgood, 1849, after a portrait by James Frothingham. Peabody first went to sea as a privateersman during the American Revolution; he was captured aboard one vessel and wounded while second mate of another, in an action "fought in his nightshirt." He began acquiring ships after the war, and by the early 19th century owned sixty-three vessels wholly or in part. He traded mainly in China, India and the East Indies, but his ships were also active in the Baltic, the Mediterranean and the West Indies. Some 7,000 seamen served aboard his merchantmen, and Peabody personally appointed thirty-five of them to the rank of master. (Peabody Museum of Salem, gift of George and Francis Peabody.)

homeward-bound from Canton, a salute was fired in her honor and most of the population of Salem put out in skiffs and rowboats to meet her and welcome her home. Later they listened spellbound to the crew's stories of fantastic Chinese manners and customs, and were curious about firecrackers, a novelty from the Orient. The *Grand Turk* was sold at great profit in the Isle de France.

The first of two principles which Derby applied to his business was to employ only the most reliable young men for his crews and to allow them an interest in the voyage. The second was to keep his smaller vessels sailing the Atlantic coast while his larger ships were in China. Or he might even send them to Europe if the price of a commodity happened to be low in this country.

As a merchant Derby was farseeing and industrious, as a citizen public-spirited and generous. The Derby mansion, which cost eighty thousand dollars to construct, was one of the most superb houses of Salem. Three stories high, it was topped with a cupola, much as was his son's house, where a deep notch cut in the window allowed an open view of the sea through a spyglass and the domed ceiling was decorated with a Corné* fresco showing the Derby fleet. He died leaving over a million dollars, a tremendous fortune in those days.

Two other prominent merchants were William Gray and Joseph Peabody. The former started in Derby's counting house and in time became one of the big shipowners, and the latter built and owned eighty-three vessels. They made thirty-eight voyages to Calcutta, seventeen to Canton, thirty-two to Sumatra, and seventy-seven to Europe. Peabody employed over seven thousand seamen who, with other Salem sailors, brought home exotic tales of remote islands, the basis for the romantic lore of the South Seas. In 1825 and 1826 the *Leander* paid on two voyages as duties the enormous sums $86,874 and $92,392 on China cargoes. It was the energy of these men and others like them that made the name of Salem familiar to the world.

In August 1783, Joseph Felt wrote, quoting the *Gazette*, that a deep interest was felt in Salem at the prospect of extending her foreign trade: "We have at an earlier period than the most sanguine Whig could have expected or even hoped, or the most

---

* The painter Michaele Felice Corné, born in Italy in 1752, died in Newport, R. I., in 1832.

inveterate Tory feared, every pleasing prospect of a very extensive commerce with the most distant parts of the Globe." But the War of 1812 tolled the knell of Salem's brilliancy, and her prosperity as a seaport came to an end in 1845. Four years later Nathaniel Hawthorne, then surveyor of the port, in his introduction to *The Scarlet Letter* described the once bustling wharf as dilapidated and languid, and the Custom House, but a short time ago the resort of activity and business, shoddy with grass growing through its chinks. A few ancient seamen loitered the streets where in the halcyon days the sea-flushed shipmaster, the vessel's papers in a cylindrical tin under his arm, made straight for the Customs, even before receiving his wife's welcome home.

As Salem's prosperity dwindled, the motto on her city seal stood for little more than tradition—*Divitis Indiae usque ad ultimum sinum*, or "To the farthest gulf of the rich East"—but if Salem lapsed into a coma in which she remembered only fitfully the great days, other Atlantic seaports were changing from market towns to centers of world commerce. The picturesque waterfronts of Boston, New York, Philadelphia and Baltimore were lined with handsome East Indiamen whose houseflags, familiar in two hemispheres, fluttered gaily in the breeze. The best residential sections ran parallel to the waterfronts, whence it was an easy step for the dignified and elegant merchants, attended, perhaps, by servants or slaves, to walk out each morning and scan the horizon for expected homecoming vessels. When a ship arrived, owner and captain made off for the counting rooms for a consultation on the probable profits. When the work of unloading was finished, blue-jacketed sailors, trim for shore leave and several months' pay to the good, swaggered the streets and turned bragadoccio under the admiring glances of gaping girls.

There were few boys in the port towns who could resist the call of the sea, and at the age of thirteen or fourteen they took their hereditary places before the mast, following in the steps of their fathers and grandfathers. But the sea was only a means to an end; every lad of ambition looked forward to the time when he would have ships of his own after serving an apprenticeship on the forecastle and in the cabin, as mate and as captain. The merchant was a respected figure in the community; he was influential in politics, the arbiter in the social life of the place and the person to whom those in want turned, and he took his responsibilities seriously. The fortunes so shrewdly amassed went not solely to family aggrandisement but also to civic improvement, to the endowment of benevolent institutions for those less fortunate—orphanages, hospitals and homes. When Lafayette visited Boston he asked, "Where are your poor?"

New Englanders were by nature cautious in money matters, but the wealth which flowed into their pockets could not but exert a change in their mode of living. That, and the fact that most of them had seen the far corners of the earth, had a mellowing influence. They did not become sybarites but gradually they learned the art of gracious living. They sipped appreciatively the Madeira their ships had carried round the world; they commissioned Bulfinch and McIntire to build their houses, Copley and Gilbert Stuart to paint their portraits, and their ship carvers executed interior woodwork with delicacy and refinement of design. Peculiar to New England were the twisted balusters and newel posts in imitation of rope form enhancing the grace and elegance of the stairways which no other artisans other than ship carvers could have so successfully executed. It was the merchants in the China trade who fostered the culture of the next generations and who were the link between the Puritans of the eighteenth century and the Intellectuals of the nineteenth century.

9

THE OPIUM WAR; AMERICAN TRADING HOUSES AND MISSIONARIES

It was to the advantage of everyone that trade in Canton should continue without interruption, but it was inevitable that incidents should occur to make this impossible, and when misunderstandings or quarrels broke out either between foreigners or foreigners and Chinese, business was at once suspended. Illustrative of this and of the Chinese jurisdiction is the case of a gunner on the British ship *Lady Hughes*.

About the same time the *Empress of China* arrived in Canton, Mr. Smith, the supercargo of the *Lady Hughes*, entertained the captain and some friends from the factories on board ship. As the guests were leaving, a salute was fired and one of the shots killed a Chinese on a mandarin's boat. According to Chinese law an eye must be given for an eye, a tooth for a tooth and a life for a life, although it was not necessarily the guilty person who was made to suffer punishment, for as long as somebody paid the penalty the Chinese felt satisfied justice had been obtained. The English chief, knowing the affair had been an accident and the gunner innocent, refused to hand over the unfortunate man to the Chinese for trial. Fresh in everyone's mind was an incident of four years before when a Frenchman had killed a Portuguese sailor in self-defense. He had acted only to save his own life and this the Chinese understood very well, but insisted on holding him for examination, and although a promise was given he would not be hurt, he was later found strangled by the waterside.

The gunner, unwilling to undergo similar punishment, took to his heels and disappeared from view and after two days' debate the Chinese told the British chief they were satisfied nothing further could be done. Everyone was greatly relieved, thinking the affair had come to an end, but far from being ended it had only begun. Pwankeiqua, under duress from the civil authorities, resorted to the ruse of sending for Mr. Smith to come to his house for a business discussion. No sooner had the supercargo arrived than he was seized by the guards and taken a prisoner to the city. As soon as this became known, all trade was stopped, the Chinese merchants retired within the city walls and the foreigners assembled to decide what course they should pursue. They determined to make it a common cause and ordered armed boats to proceed from Whampoa to the factories for protection. The boats were fired on by the Emperor's junks in passage, but only one man was wounded. In the meantime, the servants and compradores had fled so only foreigners were left in the factories, which were threatened by forty war junks drawn up on opposite sides of the river. A letter was dispatched to the co-hong declaring Mr. Smith's innocence in the affair and the impossibilty of finding the gunner, to which a reply was received the next morning stating Mr. Smith would be released when the gunner was turned over to the officials and that orders had been given for the whole force of the province to stand in readiness to attack in case of resistance.

Although the Europeans had agreed to act in unison, the Danes, French and Dutch would not go so far as to have their commerce imperilled, and when they saw the determined attitude of the authorities ordered their boats back to Whampoa. The French consul urged Major Shaw to order away the American boat, but Shaw replied he considered "the rights of humanity deeply interested in the present business" and would not dispatch the boat until the purposes for which it had been required were answered.

On the second evening more messengers arrived with word that Mr. Smith was being held only for questioning and with the request that all the foreigners except the British would come the next day to meet the Fuen. The meeting place was a pagoda; the entrance was lined with ranks of soldiers armed with scimitars through which mandarins of war escorted the supercargoes to the

Fuen. The foreign spokesman stated that the case was considered as affecting not only the British but every nationality, and that no person of property could longer be considered secure. He added it was impossible to find the gunner, to which the Fuen replied, "No matter, he must be produced." Tea was then served, each representative presented with a scarlet scroll and the interview thus being ended according to protocol, the foreigners were escorted back to their factories.

In the meantime the British had sent five boats to Whampoa to search for the missing gunner, who was eventually found and turned over to the authorities. Mr. Smith was at once released and the restrictions on trade removed. Four weeks later the *Empress of China* sailed for home and six weeks later the unhappy gunner was strangled by direct order of the Emperor. He was allowed a trial although it was completely unintelligible to him, which made the execution seem the more unjust, for according to Chinese law he could have ransomed himself for about twenty dollars. As a result of the accident on the *Lady Hughes*, the custom of saluting while in the river was entirely abolished.

There were other cases of homicide. In 1807, a party of drunken sailors put some natives to flight, killing one of them. Trade was immediately stopped and the security merchant of the ship held responsible for turning over the guilty man. In 1820, the body of a member of a ship's crew who committed suicide was given to the authorities as having been the person who killed a Chinese. In 1821, an American seaman, Francis Terranova, from the *Emily* of Baltimore, was accused of causing the death of a boatwoman who had come to trade with the sailors, by dropping a bottle on her head. Although no American believed the man should be punished, he was found guilty by the Chinese officials who tried him on board ship. The ship's guarantor was arrested and trade stopped until Terranova was handed over. A few days later he was strangled. The American merchants at Canton drew up a statement of the case which was given to Houqua to present to the Viceroy. In it was stated, "We are bound to submit to your laws while we are in your waters; be they ever so unjust we will not resist them." The American government took no notice of the affair whatsoever, either to investigate or remonstrate, nor could the consul, without backing from home and not recognized as an official by the Chinese, offer any protestation. The provincial officials held a powerful weapon: merely by stopping trade, they forced the foreigners to conform to the archaic laws of the Empire.

It was a series of incidents such as the above, quite aside from any question of opium, which finally decided the British Parliament to send troops to China to protect their nationals, an action which has passed into history with the lamentable epithet of the "Opium War."

In their laws the Chinese made no discrimination against the foreigners; natives, too, suffered the same punishments, but the cases cited illustrate the insecure position held by the Europeans and Americans in Canton. Without the assistance of interpreters and with no knowledge of Chinese jurisdiction, they were forced to submit to trials of which they could not understand a word.

Anxious to put trade relations on a more favorable footing, the British government sent two missions to Peking, the first in 1794 under Earl Macartney, and the second in 1816 under Lord Amherst. Lord Amherst and his suite were never received owing to the fact they refused to perform the kowtow. Of the Macartney mission little is known regarding its impression on the Chinese, although judging from the "mandate" sent by Ch'ien Lung to George III, quoted in part in Chapter I, it would seem the Son of Heaven regarded it as one of the most splendid tribute-bearing embassies ever sent by a vassal state to acknowledge humble obeisance to the great Emperor!

From the time the first American ships sailed up the Pearl River until the beginning of the Opium War, there were few changes in foreign relations at Canton. As the American-East India trade became established, the services of supercargoes were gradually replaced by firms and commission houses. The first American firm in China, that of Shaw and Randall, was short lived due to the death of Major Shaw, who succumbed to a complaint of the liver in his fortieth year on a voyage home. His untimely death was a great loss to the country he served so well, both in war and in peace, and which he represented abroad with such dignity and distinction.

In 1803, the firm of Perkins and Co., a branch of J. and T. H. Perkins of Boston, was founded. Other well-known firms were Olyphant and Co., Russell and Co., Bryant and Sturgis, and the houses of Heard and Wetmore. Eventually Perkins and Co., James P. Sturgis and Co., and Russell and Sturgis of Manila were amalgamated into the one firm of Russell and Co., which became the most important American concern in Canton. The success of the house was due largely to the friendship and influence of Houqua and to their relations with Baring Brothers of London. When the Honorable East India Company's long monopoly at Canton came to an end, Houqua withdrew from general business and devoted his energies exclusively to Russell and Co. Through them his foreign affairs were managed, and on their ships were sent the celebrated Chops of Congou, which were grown on his family estates in Woo-E and were well known and enjoyed in Europe and America.

Two young men to make fortunes in the employ of Russell and Co. were John Perkins Cushing and his cousin, Robert Bennet Forbes, nephews of the founders. Owing to the illness of the chief, the affairs of the Canton firm fell into Cushing's hands when he was only sixteen, but he seemed to have such a thorough grasp of the business in spite of his youth that his uncles took him into partnership. He stayed in China for thirty years, became an intimate friend of the great Houqua and was trusted and admired by both Chinese and foreigners alike. He returned to Boston a wealthy man, but he could not altogether dissociate himself from the East for he surrounded his house and gardens with a high wall, like the houses of the rich in China, and was waited on by a retinue of Chinese servants who, although in a western land, clung to their native garb. His house was filled with oriental art and bibelots.

Robert Forbes went to sea at the age of thirteen. In his *Reminiscences*, he wrote, "Beginning in 1817, with a capital consisting of a Testament, a 'Bowditch', a quadrant, a chest of sea clothes, and a mother's blessing, I left the paternal mansion full of hope and good resolutions, and the promise of support from my uncles. At the age of sixteen, I filled a man's place as third mate; at the age of twenty, I was promoted to a command; at the age of twenty-six, I commanded my own ship; at twenty-eight I abandoned the sea as a profession; at thirty-six I was head of the largest American house at Canton." Forbes' buoyant personality, his charm and frankness all made it easy for him to take Cushing's place in Canton as the number one American taipan.

In the second decade of the nineteenth century, two extraordinary occurrences took place, both almost unprecedented in the annals of foreign trade at Canton. The first was an embezzlement by one of the compradores in the American factory, who used company funds for his own speculation. He had been

Robert Bennet Forbes (1804-89), building ship models in his retirement years at Milton, Mass. In his Personal Reminiscences, *he wrote: "Beginning in 1817, with a capital consisting of a Testament, a 'Bowditch', a quadrant, a chest of sea clothes, and a mother's blessing, I left the paternal mansion full of hope and good resolutions, and the promise of support from my uncles [one of whom was his mother's brother, Colonel T. H. Perkins]. At the age of sixteen, I filled a man's place as third mate; at the age of twenty, I was promoted to a command; at the age of twenty-six, I commanded my own ship; at twenty-eight I abandoned the sea as a profession; at thirty-six I was head of the largest American house at Canton."*

After nearly a decade of retirement in Boston, Forbes was in China again as head of Russell & Company from 1849 to 1851, serving also as American and French vice-consul. According to the Dictionary of American Biography, *"by that time, he had entered the third state of his career, that of ship-owner. Altogether, he was connected with sixty-eight vessels as part owner or supervisor of construction. He invented the 'Forbes rig' for sailing vessels, described as 'a pole topmast fiddling abaft,' later improved and patented by Howes. He was among the first to have faith in the screw propeller and iron hulls. . . He was always interested in humanitarian work. In 1847, he commanded the* U.S.S. Jamestown, *loaned to carry contributions from Boston to the Irish famine sufferers. He jumped into the sea to make daring rescues after a collision in 1849. He energetically supported coastal lifesaving work, nautical training ships and sailors' homes . . . He was always an enthusiastic sportsman. He was 'commodore' of the first informal yacht club in Boston, and at sixty-five he took up fox hunting at Pau. He is said to have had unusual personal charm."*

Houqua (1769-1843), mezzotint by John Sartain after a portrait by George Chinnery in the collection of Benjamin Chew Wilcocks of Philadelphia. Houqua was the senior hong merchant of Canton and a staunch friend of the American merchants there. During the latter part of his career, Houqua devoted his energies exclusively to Russell and Co., and managed his foreign ventures through that house—including substantial investments in the infant U. S. railroad industry. (Peabody Museum of Salem; photograph by Mark Sexton.)

recommended by Houqua and therefore the American chief reported the loss of money to that merchant. The compradore was sent for and confessed to having taken fifty thousand dollars which he intended to replace but was detected before he had the chance. Houqua at once covered the deficiency.

The second strange event was the arrival at the factories of several English and American ladies in direct defiance of regulations. This thoroughly embarrassed the members of the co-hong, who were at their wits' end with such an unheard of thing and ordered the ladies to leave at once else the Son of Heaven "so considerate for all beyond the seas would withdraw his compassion." To the great relief of the co-hong, the ladies decided to depart after a few days and were escorted to their boat by the gentlemen of the factories. For this occasion coats which had been stored in camphor ten or fifteen years, old-fashioned cravats and dingy white gloves suddenly came to light, although one or two inveterate bachelors complained at such useless fuss and bother.

Because of trade, American interest in China was constantly increasing. By the turn of the century, the Church exhibited an awakening interest in this new field, although the propagation of Christianity was still a dangerous affair and was not permitted within the borders of the Empire. Furthermore, the British East India Company, unwilling to have anything interfere with trade, discountenanced the idea of Englishmen coming to Canton to spread the Gospel. Nevertheless, the first Protestant missionary was an Englishman, Dr. Robert Morrison, who arrived in Canton in 1807 by way of New York, having been refused passage on a company ship. The Secretary of State, James Madison, gave him a letter to Consul Carrington requesting any assistance possible, and for a while Dr. Morrison lived at the American factory with Messrs. Milner and Bull of New York. After a time he made the acquaintance of Sir George Staunton and Mr. Roberts of the British factory, and in 1808 he was forced to flee with them and other of his compatriots to Macao. In that year the British, afraid of an attack on the island, landed troops to aid the Portuguese. The Chinese, infuriated with interference in their own territory, at once stopped trade with the British and refused to supply their ships at Whampoa. When the British troops withdrew from Macao and returned to India, trade was resumed.

Doctor Morrison became translator for the East India Company and his association with that powerful organization undoubtedly gave him a footing in China he would not otherwise have had. In 1814, a Chinese edition of the New Testament appeared, a large part of it Morrison's work.

American Protestants were eager to follow the example of British churches and in 1830 the Reverend David Abeel and the Reverend Elijah Bridgman arrived in Canton. They were given free passage and a year's residence by D. W. C. Olyphant of the firm of Olyphant and Co. Because of the stringency of Chinese laws regarding the diffusion of Christianity, work was confined mostly to language study and translation. Missions were started in Malacca, Singapore, Penang, Borneo and Batavia to afford, Americans and Europeans the opportunity of learning Chinese from emigrés living in those places, and whatever was done in Canton was done as quietly as possible. The Reverend Bridgman, backed by Olyphant, who guaranteed expenses, started a periodical called *The Chinese Repository* for the dissemination of knowledge concerning the history, laws, culture and customs of the Chinese.

The interest of the Church, the reports of the merchants and the fact that the United States was now an established nation and Americans could turn their thoughts outward rather than toward any immediate problem of their own, all were contributing factors to the growing interest in China. She was regarded with respect, with envy even, and Jefferson extolled her non-intercourse with other nations as ideal. It was the fashion of the day to drink fragrant Chinese tea, to dine from the delicate willow pattern ware and to enjoy the other luxuries which came from this country of ancient civilization.

At the beginning of the Opium War, American sympathy was all with the Chinese, and cartoons even went so far as to present the picture of Englishmen forcing the drug down powerless natives' throats at sword's point. It was John Quincy Adams who startled Americans by advancing the theory that the cause of the war was not opium, but "the kowtow—the arrogant and the insupportable pretensions of China." The seizure of opium, he said, was a mere incident to the dispute and had no more to do with the war than the Boston Tea Party had to do with the American Revolution. Gradually the picture changed, people no longer thought of unwilling Chinese being forcibly drugged, and with China's complete collapse before British arms, the impression spread that she was a nation falling into decay. It was not to China's discredit, however, that she was inferior in military strategy, a calling long despised by the sages, nor did her surrender mean her civilization had come to an end. The war was inevitable and it was fought because China for years had blandly ignored her true position in relation to the nations of the West; for centuries conqueror, ruler, despot of the East, she refused to acknowledge equality in any quarter of the globe.

That was the underlying cause of the dispute. What brought it to a head was that neither foreigners nor Chinese at Canton took seriously the Imperial edicts from the Court at Peking.

From time to time viceroys and magistrates deemed it their duty to issue proclamations, "but," wrote W. C. Hunter, "we disregarded local orders as well as those from Peking and really became confident that we should enjoy perpetual immunity as far as the opium trade was concerned."

The drug arrived in British bottoms from India, in American bottoms from Turkey, store ships lay outside Cap-Sing-Moon and Lintin and not only "smug-boats," but even mandarin boats sent out to put an end to the smuggling, ran the drug into Canton. In 1826, Forbes commanded a ship up the coast having on board a cargo of opium but was forced to return to Canton before contacting merchants, much against the wishes of the rest of the party who had expected to make an immense profit. W. C. Hunter sailed to Nan'ao on another Russell vessel and has left the following description of how opium was sold along the coast:

> Knowing the formalities to be gone through with the mandarins we expected a visit from one and until it was made no Chinese boat would come alongside, nor would a junk, not even a bumboat. We had no sooner furled sails and made everything shipshape when his 'Excellency' appeared in his gig, a sort of scow as broad as she was long. Besides the oarsmen there were official and personal attendants, in grass cloth with conical rattan hats and flowing red silk cords surrounding them to the brim. He himself sat majestically in an arm chair smoking quietly. A large embroidered silk umbrella was held over his head, while servants with fans protected him from the attack of mosquitoes and flies. He was received at the gangway by Captain Forster. His manner and bearing were easy and dignified. When cheroots and a glass of wine had been offered, the 'commodore' inquired the cause of our anchoring at Nan'ao. The schroff gave him to understand that the vessel being on her way from Singapore to Canton had been compelled, through contrary winds and currents, to replenish her wood and water. Having listened attentively the great man said that any supplies might be obtained, but

when they were on board not a moment was to be lost in sailing for Whampoa, as the great Emperor did not permit vessels from afar to visit any other port. He then gravely pulled from his boot a red document and handed it to his secretary.

The document stated that the Son of Heaven in all his mercy could not deny succor to those who were in want of food.

This formality being over with [continued Hunter], and wine drunk, we proceeded to business. The mandarin opened by the direct question, 'How many chests have you on board?' . . . And then came the question of cumshaw and that was settled on the good old Chinese principle of 'allee same custom.' . . . Chinese buyers came on board freely the moment they saw the official visit had been paid.

For years British merchants had been petitioning their government to grant them the privilege of free trade so that they might compete with Americans. At length the ban was lifted, and the British East India Company dissolved in 1834. In the same year Lord Napier, a former officer in the Navy who had served under Nelson, arrived in Canton to assume the office of Government Superintendent of Trade and as such was a representative of the Crown. The British considered the change of some importance, but to the Chinese, Napier was simply another merchant or "headman" and the officials refused to receive him except through the ordinary channels—i.e., a letter in the form of a respectful petition presented through the co-hong—because to do so would be to acknowledge England the equal of China. Lord Napier refused to deal through the co-hong, or, as he was ordered to do by the Chinese, to withdraw from Canton. In this dilemma, affairs came to a deadlock and, as always, trade was stopped. Weeks passed, nothing was accomplished, and finally Lord Napier decided to leave for Macao. He was not in good health at the time and the strain of his mission was too much for him. He died shortly after his arrival at the island.

In the meantime, the opium trade was flourishing and the provincial authorities were making no real effort to stop it, although the Court at Peking was sincere in its desire to curb importation. The unhappy Emperor lamented, "How can I die and meet the spirits of my Imperial ancestors unless these direful evils are removed?"

The burning question was whether or not to legalize the traffic, a question of great import to both Chinese and foreigners. Memorials were sent to the Emperor on the subject but in the end he determined to make an even more strenuous effort to suppress the trade. Unfortunate smokers were subjected to torture as an example, yet the son of the governor of Canton was engaged in the commerce!

In 1839, the government, not only alarmed by the noxious effect on the people, but seriously concerned at the amount of specie going out of the country, determined to put an end to opium smuggling. Lin Tse-hsü was ordered by the Emperor to proceed to Canton and to adopt any measures he saw fit to stop the scourge. Robert Forbes said, "He struck directly at the head and front of the offending. Without any warning in advance, Lin made his appearance on the 10th of March and on the 19th he issued a proclamation demanding of the foreign community the instant delivery of every chest of opium within the waters of China! The hong merchants through whom all legitimate trade was conducted were threatened with immediate death if the Imperial mandate was not immediately obeyed."

This swift and direct action, so unlike the usual tortuous Chinese methods, came indeed as a surprise, while Lin, further to emphasize his demands, threw a cordon of armed boats across the waterfront. He denied permission to any foreigners to leave the city and ordered all servants, compradores and coolies to quit their foreign employers. The merchants were virtual prisoners in their own factories.

At this critical moment, Captain Elliot, British Superintendent of Trade, arrived from Macao and called on all his countrymen, in the name of Her Majesty the Queen, to surrender whatever opium they might have. Twenty thousand, two hundred and eighty-three chests were handed over, amounting in value to nearly nine million dollars. Despite the doubt of some, that after the drug was seized trade would be legalized, every bit of it was destroyed by emptying it into trenches of water which were afterward directed into the river. One poor wretch was decapitated for trying to salvage an infinitesimal amount.

In spite of the seriousness of the situation, it was not without its lighter side. Chinese government officials sent presents of pigs, fowl and sheep to the factories so there was no food shortage, but as the servants had been ordered to leave, the foreigners were compelled to take care of themselves.

"In the American hong," wrote Robert Forbes, "lived Mr. W. P. Snow, United States consul, Russell and Co., Russell, Sturgis and Co., and others. I was called upon to organize the house for work; lots were drawn to see who should cook, and who should play the part of waiters, chambermen, etc. It fell upon me to be the chief cook. The first thing to be done was to clean out the kitchen, into which no white man had before entered; all hands went at it, and soon made things fit for my new work. My first effort was fried ham and eggs; when the dish came to the table it was difficult to distinguish between the eggs and the ham; all bore the color and partook of the consistency of dirty shoe leather. It was immediately voted to depose me, and to put Warren Delano* in my place, and I assumed his duties, which were to look after the glass and silver; to this end I put upon the sideboard a piece of sheeting, and when I required towels I had only to tear off a strip, wipe my utensils, and throw the strip into the corner. . . Bathing was important, and no coolie at hand to carry water to the upper rooms, we rigged whips and attempted to hoist the big pails into the verandahs; but this proved a failure, the ropes twisted up, and the pails remained suspended in midair. The venerable consul mourned much over this state of durance vile, and lamented his hard fate. One morning I met him on the stairs, intent on some household errand, when he opened his heart to me in this wise: 'Is it not too bad, Mr. Forbes, that a public official at my time of life, not owning a pound of opium, should be imprisoned, and compelled to do chambermaid's work?'"

The chauvinist Lin, not content with having destroyed the opium and still firm in the belief that he held the foreigners in the hollow of his hand through the simple expedient of stopping trade—like all Chinese he was convinced the "outer barbarians" would suffer any indignity rather than lose their profits in teas and silks—took it upon himself to rebuke Queen Victoria for the conduct of her subjects:

You savages of the farther seas have waxed so bold, it seems, as to defy and insult our mighty Empire. Of a truth it is high time to 'flay the face and cleanse the heart' and to amend your ways. If you submit humbly to the Celestial dynasty and tender your allegiance, it may give you a chance to purge yourself of your past sins. But if you persist and

* Maternal grandfather of President Franklin Delano Roosevelt.

continue in your path of obstinate delusion, your three islands will be laid waste and your people pounded into mincemeat, so soon as the armies of his Divine Majesty set foot upon your shores.*

After the confiscation and the destruction of the opium the British to a man deserted the factories for Macao. Captain Elliot begged the Americans to follow him.

"If your house goes all will go," he said to Forbes, "and we shall bring these rascally Chinese to terms."

Forbes replied he had not come to China for his health or his pleasure, that the Yankees had no Queen to guarantee their losses, and that he should remain at his post as long as he could sell a yard of goods or buy a pound of tea.

Lin was nonplussed at the action of the British, but he was sure that sooner or later they would return to Canton for their cargoes. Nor, it seemed, did his stringent measures prevent smuggling; although the large houses had signed bonds never again to import opium, the small merchants were not too scrupulous to seize this opportunity for enormous profit. The destruction of all the opium in Canton had increased its value immeasurably! The situation may be compared to our own during the era of Prohibition, but, where the United States was prepared to back up the law with a powerful coast guard, the Chinese dealt in futile threats and empty words.

The British were forced from Macao to the island of Hong Kong, where skirmishing took place between their vessels and the Chinese. In those days means of communication were slow but everyone knew that sooner or later England would seek redress for the imprisonment of her nationals during the opium confiscation. Even the Chinese seemed to feel that some reprisal would be made—they were not ignorant of the continual and rapid conquests made by the British all over India—and they began to muster their troops and repair their forts.

The great problem was to remove British goods piled up in their factories to British ships before hostilities actually commenced. The Yankees were not slow to seize this chance. Freights skyrocketed: five to seven dollars a bale on teas and silks for the ninety-mile trip was more than was paid for freight from China to America! All available craft were pressed into service, were loaded to overflowing, and when Captain Elliot

* Backhouse and Bland.

later met Forbes at Macao he said to him, "My dear Forbes, the Queen owes you many thanks for not taking my advice as to leaving Canton. We have got in all our goods and got out a full supply of teas and silks. . . . Now the season is over and a large force at hand we can bring the Chinese to terms."

Fifteen months after Commissioner Lin seized all the foreign-owned opium in Canton, British troops arrived in China. That there could be but one result was obvious to everyone except His Imperial Majesty and his sycophants who still clung to their belief in the omnipotence of the Celestial Empire. That the Chinese warriors were brave was proved, but China, convinced of her own superiority for centuries, suddenly discovered that the matchlocks, bows and arrows of her infantry were of little avail against a relatively small but well-equipped and well-trained body of English soldiers. The grand armies of the Son of Heaven, as in Alice's dream, turned out to be as harmless as a deck of cards!

The Emperor was finally prevailed upon to appoint three commissioners to settle the terms of peace. The three men were Ilipu, Niu Kien and Kiyeng, who met Sir Henry Pottinger, the British Plenipotentiary, at Nanking in August of 1842. The Treaty of Nanking stipulated that the ports of Amoy, Foochow, Ningpo and Shanghai be opened to trade and to residence; that the island of Hong Kong be ceded for the purpose of careening ships; that British nationals were no longer under Chinese jurisdiction; and that six million dollars be paid for the opium destroyed; three million to merchants on account of debts; and twelve million to the British Government for expenses incurred in the war. The Imperial Commissioners, to soothe the vanity of the Son of Heaven, memorialized him explaining that this sum of twenty-one million dollars was to be paid partly because of debts incurred by the co-hong and partly as a present to the British soldiers and sailors before sending them home.

The Treaty of Nanking also provided for the abolition of all monopolies and thus came to an end the duties of that honorable body of merchants, the co-hong.

10

THE TREATY OF WANGHIA; THE SWAN SONG OF THE AMERICAN CHINA TRADE

The next negotiation entered into between China and a foreign power was the Treaty of Wanghia, drawn up in 1844 by the Honorable Caleb Cushing, Massachusetts lawyer and Envoy Extraordinary of the United States, and Kiyeng, Imperial Commissioner, Governor General of the two Kwang Provinces, Vice Guardian of the Heir Apparent and Superintendent of trade and foreign intercourse of the Five Ports.

During the Opium War, Boston and Salem merchants had asked Congress for naval protection from pirates in Chinese waters and had received it in the East India Squadron under the command of Commodore Kearny, who arrived at Canton with the *Constellation* and the *Boston* in 1842. Diplomat as well as officer, Kearny maintained friendly relations with both the English and the Chinese and wrote home to urge that a mission be sent out to arrange a treaty guaranteeing Americans equal privileges with the British.

American merchants in China were quite willing to continue business without any formal agreement between the two countries, but at home public opinion had been aroused and much was made of the fact that, although England had opened up the Celestial Empire, there was no reason to suppose other nations would be allowed entrance in the treaty ports. If America were to continue her trade on a par with the British it was essential she make her own arrangements. The State Department sent out a circular letter asking for suggestions from those familiar with China, and from some Boston merchants came the following advice:

> The Chinese want no political intercourse with foreign nations, and they will only permit it through fear of armed compulsion, or through a politic desire to offer us *voluntarily* what has been *forced* on them by others. . . . If our envoy does not see his way clear to succeed let him do nothing. . . . We repeat our firm conviction that he can only do mischief by attempting to gain any point by negotiation which the Chinese are not ready to grant.

The merchants wanted a treaty only if it would not antagonize the Chinese and thus nullify the privileges they already enjoyed!

Edward Everett, then Minister to London, was approached on the subject of heading the mission, but declined the nomination, which was finally offered to Caleb Cushing. Cushing was a friend of both President Tyler and Daniel Webster. It is true that he was often ridiculed for his mannerisms and peculiarity of dress, but his legal training and his shrewd New England mind were a match for any wily Oriental and the treaty which he was able to draw up served as a model for all treaties for many years. Before he sailed, he attended a dinner in Faneuil Hall in Boston, in company with President Tyler and Daniel Webster, and in a speech said, "I have been entrusted with a commission of peace and with the duty of bringing nearer together, if possible, the civilization of the old and new worlds. . . For though of old, it was from the East that civilization and learning dawned upon the world, yet now, by the refluent tide of letters, knowledge is being rolled back from West to East, and we have become the teachers of our teachers. I go to China. . . that, if possible, the doors of three hundred millions of Asiatic laborers may be opened to America."

Although there was opposition in Congress to the mission because of the expense such an undertaking would involve, a salary was voted Cushing and an appropriation made for outfitting the embassy. Four warships were ordered as escort: the new frigate *Missouri*, pride of the Navy, the frigate *Brandywine*, the sloop-of-war *St. Louis*, and the brig *Perry*. Cushing, having ordered the uniform of a major-general, "a blue coat with gilt buttons, embroidered, a white satin vest, white pantaloons with a gold stripe down the seam and a chapeau with white plumes," set forth on his journey accompanied by

Fletcher Webster as secretary, Elisha Kane, surgeon, and five voluntary attachés serving without pay for the experience.

The magnificent uniform was destined never to be worn, for at Gibraltar the *Missouri* burst into flames and although Cushing, who was on shore, rushed to the burning vessel he was able to save only the official papers. After this disaster he decided to go overland to Suez and from there to Bombay, where the rest of his mission met him.

Cushing's instructions from the State Department were to make the Chinese understand, first of all, that the intentions of the embassy were entirely peaceful and simply to insure friendly intercourse between the two nations; that the Americans were not seeking territorial possessions or concessions, but only the privileges already granted the British of trading at Amoy, Ningpo, Foochow and Shanghai as well as Canton. Secondly, he was to proceed to Peking if possible and request an audience with the Emperor. If this were granted, he was not to perform the kowtow under any circumstances whatsoever, nor were any presents to be given lest they be misconstrued as tribute offerings. The Emperor was to be treated with the same deference any European sovereign would receive from an American ambassador.

Apparently the reason for wanting Cushing to go to Peking was that he might present in person to the Son of Heaven a letter from the President. The authorship of the letter has been attributed to Daniel Webster, though he had resigned as secretary of state, but it seems more probable that it was drafted by some clerk who ignorantly placed Chinese in the same category with savages and Indians. That the letter was sent at all seems curious; it was scarcely fit for the President to address the omnipotent ruler of ancient Cathay in such singular language as follows:

LETTER TO THE EMPEROR OF CHINA FROM THE PRESIDENT OF THE UNITED STATES OF AMERICA

I, John Tyler, President of the United States of America which states are: Maine, New Hampshire, Massachusetts, Rhode Island, Connecticut, Vermont, New York, New Jersey, Pennsylvania, Delaware, Maryland, Virginia, North Carolina, South Carolina, Georgia, Kentucky, Tennessee, Ohio, Louisiana, Indiana, Mississippi, Illinois, Alabama, Missouri, Arkansas, and Michigan, send you this letter of peace and friendship signed with my own hand.

I hope your health is good. China is a great Empire extending over a great part of the world. The Chinese are numerous. You have millions and millions of subjects. The twenty-six United States are as large as China, though our people are not so numerous. The rising sun looks upon the great rivers and great mountains of China. When he sets he looks upon rivers and mountains equally large in the United States. Our territories extend from one great ocean to the other; and on the west we are divided from your dominions only by the sea. Leaving the mouth of one of our great rivers, and going constantly toward the setting sun, we sail to Japan and the Yellow Sea.

Now, my words are that the governments of two such great countries should be at peace. It is proper and according to the will of Heaven, that they should respect each other, and act wisely. I therefore send to your court Count Caleb Cushing, one of the wise and learned men of this country. On his first arrival in China he will inquire of your health. He has strict orders to go to your great city of Peking, and there to deliver this letter. He will have with him secretaries and interpreters.

The Chinese love to trade with our people and sell them tea and silk, for which our people pay silver and sometimes other articles. But if the Chinese and Americans will trade, there shall be rules, so that they shall not break your laws or our laws. Our Minister, Caleb Cushing, is authorized to make a treaty to regulate trade. Let it be just. Let there be no unfair advantage on either side. Let the people trade not only at Canton, but also at Amoy, Ningpo, Shanghai and Fuchow, and all such other places as may offer profitable exchanges both to China and the United States, provided they do not break your laws. Therefore, we doubt not you will be pleased our messenger of peace, with this letter in his hand, shall come to Peking and there deliver it; and that your great officers will, by your orders, make a treaty with him to regulate the terms of trade—so that nothing may happen to disturb the peace between China and America. Let the treaty be signed by your own Imperial hand. It shall be signed by mine, by the authority of our great council, the Senate.

And so may your health be good and peace reign.

Written at Washington this twelfth day of July, in the year of our Lord one thousand eight hundred and forty-three. Your good friend,

(Many years later E. T. Williams, a member of the international committee to examine the archives at the Chinese Foreign Office after the Boxer Rebellion of 1900, found copies of the correspondence between China and the United States. The documents, in a dusty heap on the floor, were bound in purple plush with a silver seal of the United States attached.)

After Cushing's mission had arrived at Macao, the staff was augmented by two interpreters, Reverend E. C. Bridgman and

View of the Bund, Shanghai, c. 1855, by Chow Kwa (active 1850-80). Located near the chief tea, silk and cotton producing areas of China and linked to the commerce of the Yangtze River valley, Shanghai grew from a small fishing village in 1842 into China's largest Treaty Port by 1860. (Peabody Museum of Salem, gift of the estate of Mrs. Helen Field Parker; photograph by Mark Sexton.)

Samqua (active 1825-60), oil portrait by Lam Qua, c. 1850. This is one of a group of five portraits of Cantonese merchants painted for Augustine Heard of Ipswich, Mass., and exhibited at the Boston Athenaeum in 1851. Lam Qua's work was also exhibited at the Royal Academy in London. In his book The China Trade, *Carl Crossman writes: "Lam Qua is known to have studied and lived with [the English painter George Chinnery] in the 1820's, and his Chinese student was to become the most prominent of the Chinese painters working in the English manner." (Peabody Museum of Salem.)*

Reverend Peter Parker. One wonders with what emotion they translated the President's letter, especially as their years in China had given them a keen insight into the etiquette and propriety of the Chinese people!

Cushing's first official act was to send a communication to the acting Governor-General of Canton, Ching, informing him that he had arrived at Macao, where he would remain a few weeks before proceeding to Peking. To this a reply was received stating it would be quite unnecessary for the Americans to go north because the Imperial Commissioner was already on his way south. The Chinese were determined to keep Cushing away from the capital. Weeks were spent in the exchange of diplomatic notes but at last Kiyeng arrived in Canton. In his first message to the American minister the title of "Chinese Government" stood one line higher in column than that of the "United States Government" and this Cushing immediately returned. It was sent back with the necessary correction. Next, the Imperial Commissioner stated flatly that if Cushing insisted on going to Peking he, Kiyeng, was not authorized to continue with the negotiations, and on this point Cushing yielded.

The treaty was signed at Wanghia, just outside Macao, on July 3rd, 1844, four and a half months after the arrival of the mission, with the preliminary agreement that "there shall be perfect, permanent, universal peace, and a sincere and cordial amity between the United States of America on the one part and the Ta Tsing Empire on the other part, and between their people respectively, without exception of persons or places."

Great Britain had opened the door to the China trade with the Treaty of Nanking providing that British subjects might trade at the four additional ports, that equality was to be observed in diplomatic correspondence, that all monopolies were to be dissolved, and that tonnage dues were to be lowered. These stipulations were included in the Treaty of Wanghia also, but the American treaty was more explicit and in some particulars an improvement over the British treaty. Regulations governing trade were carefully defined and included the privilege of remaining two days at any port without payment of duties if cargo were not discharged; duties were to be paid at one port only and goods might be reshipped without extra charges. Provisions concerning extraterritoriality were contained in Article XXI,

Subjects of China who may be guilty of any criminal act towards citizens of the United States shall be arrested and punished by the Chinese authorities according to the laws of China; and citizens of the United States who may commit any crime in China shall be subject to be tried and punished only by the Consul, or other public functionary of the United States, thereto authorized, according to the laws of the United States.

—and in Article XXV,

All questions in regard to rights, whether of property or person, arising between citizens of the United States and China shall be subject to jurisdiction and regulated by the authorities of their own government; and all controversies occurring in China between citizens of the United States and subjects of any other government shall be regulated by the treaties existing between the United States and such governments, respectively, without interference on the part of China.

Of importance to missionaries as well as to merchants was Article XVIII, which stated that teachers might be employed by the Chinese and books bought. Also, Americans were to be allowed to build houses, hospitals and churches, and to engage pilots, compradores, linguists, seamen and servants without interference on the part of local officials. The last Article, XXXIV, provided that the treaty might be revised after twelve years.

While Cushing was waiting in Macao for Kiyeng to arrive in Canton, an incident occurred which, because of the anti-foreign feeling of the populace, could have assumed serious proportions. The *Brandywine* brought out a new flagstaff and weathervane for the consulate which were duly erected, but the weathervane had to be removed because the natives thought it had a destructive influence and was causing disease. A mob attacked the consulate, though no serious damage was done. A few days later some Chinese assaulted some Americans and in the mêlée a Chinese was killed. The affair was referred to Cushing and Kiyeng, and Cushing insisted that the man who was responsible for the death be tried according to American law. He was acquitted on the grounds of self-defense. Kiyeng, to smooth over and hush up the matter, compensated the dead man's family for their loss.

In celebration of the signing of the treaty, the Imperial Commissioner entertained the American mission at a lavish feast, the food and wines being of the rarest. The next morning,

Cushing admitted to a "slight langour." Cushing and Kiyeng parted on amicable terms, having settled the relations between their two countries according to protocol, but if the Americans had assumed the Chinese were ignorant barbarians, the compliment was returned twofold. During the second Sino-British war, official Chinese papers were found in which Kiyeng referred to Cushing as the "Uncivilized Envoy" and told how his "stupid ignorance" had to be dispelled.

The third treaty to complete the opening of China was with France. It was based on the Treaty of Wanghia, with the additional privilege of the toleration of Christianity, both Catholic and Protestant. The Emperor wrote with his vermilion brush, "Let it be as Kiyeng says," and accordingly the Commissioner issued a statement that Chinese practicing Christianity would be held blameless and would not be subject to punishment. These treaties, humiliating to China, marked the end of an era. Gone forever was the immemorial, mysterious seclusion of an age-old civilization. The Dragon, rudely wakened from his sleep of centuries, fled.

The swan song of the American East India trade began about the time the treaties were signed and culminated with the outbreak of the American Civil War. In those years the famous clippers were developed that made our merchant marine superior to any afloat. The decline in trade was due partly to the war, but more to the change from wood to iron ships for which we were not prepared. In thinking of the old China trade, one must pay homage to the men who fostered it, to their courage and determination that American commerce should proceed unmolested throughout the world. To the ships they sailed in, John Greenleaf Whittier has written:

> God bless her! whereso'er the breeze
> Her snowy wings shall fan,
> Aside the frozen Hebrides
> Or sultry Hindostan!
> Where'er, in mart or on the main,
> With peaceful flag unfurled,
> She helps to wind the silken chain
> Of commerce round the world! . . .
> Her pathway on the open main
> May blessings follow free,
> And glad hearts welcome back again
> Her white sails from the sea!

Colonel Thomas Handasyd Perkins (1764-1854), oil portrait by Thomas Sully, commissioned in 1831 by the Boston Athenaeum, of which Perkins was then president. In his Editor's Foreword to Merchant Prince of Boston *(Harvard University Press, 1971), Ralph Hidy wrote that Colonel Perkins "was the businessman par excellence of his time. From a beginning of two small legacies and a position as an apprentice clerk in a retail establishment he amassed a fortune of more than a million dollars, largely in the China trade but also through investments in mining, iron-making, quarrying, hotels, and theaters, to mention a few. . . Wherever profit beckoned the merchant followed, whether to slaves and sugar in Santo-Domingo or opium, sea otters, and tea in Batavia and Canton. . .*

"An active Federalist, he was one of the three men who carried the views of the Hartford Convention to Washington in 1815. An early participant in local militia organizations, he also won elective office on occasion. Numerous projects won his public support, often financial as well; among them were the initial move to fill in the Back Bay, the Bunker Hill Monument, the Museum of Fine Arts, and the Massachusetts General Hospital. Of all the Perkins philanthropies undoubtedly the best known remains the Perkins Institute for the Blind."(Boston Athenaeum.)

BIBLIOGRAPHY

A. References cited by the author

Backhouse, Sir Edmund Trelawny, and John Otway Percy Bland. *Annals and Memoirs of the Court of Peking from the 16th to the 20th Century.* Boston and New York: Houghton Mifflin Company, 1914. [But see Hugh Trevor-Roper, *The Hermit of Peking,* in Section B below.]

Boit, John. "Log of the *Columbia,* 1790-92." In the *Proceedings of theMassachusetts Historical Society,* vol. LIII, 217-275. Boston: 1920.

Day, Clive. *A History of Commerce of the United States.* New ed., rev. and enl. New York: Longmans, Green & Company, 1926.

Delano, Amasa. *A Narrative of Voyages and Travels in Northern and Southern Hemispheres.* Boston: E. G. House, 1817.

Dennett, Tyler. *Americans in Eastern Asia; a Cultural Study of the Policy of the United States with Reference to China, Japan and Korea in the 19th century.* New York: The Macmillan Company, 1922.

Dulles, Foster Rhea. *The Old China Trade.* Boston and New York: Houghton Mifflin Company, 1930.

Fanning, Captain Edmund. *Voyages and Discoveries in the South Seas, 1792-1832.* Salem: Marine Research Society, 1924.

Felt, Joseph B. *Annals of Salem, from Its First Settlement.* Salem: W. & S. B. Ives, 1827.

Forbes, Robert Bennet. *Personal Reminiscences.* 2nd ed., rev. Boston: Little, Brown, 1882.

Fuess, Claude M. *The Life of Caleb Cushing,* New York: Harcourt, Brace & Company, 1923.

Gilbert, Rodney. *The Unequal Treaties. China and The Foreigner.* London: John Murray, 1929.

Greenbie, Sydney, and Marjorie Barstow Greenbie. *Gold of Ophir; or the Lure That Made America.* New York: Doubleday, Doran & Company, Inc., 1925.

Hamilton, Alexander. *Industrial and Commercial Correspondence of Alexander Hamilton, Anticipating His Report on Manufactures.* Edited by Arthur Harrison Cole. Chicago: A. W. Shaw Company, 1928.

Hunter, William C. *Bits of Old China.* London: K. Paul, Trench & Co., 1885.

——. *The 'Fan Kwae' at Canton Before Treaty Days.* London: K. Paul, Trench & Co., 1882.

Jewitt, John Rodgers. *Narrative of the Adventures and Sufferings of John R. Jewitt.* Middletown, Conn.: Loomis & Richards, 1815.

Latourette, Kenneth Scott. *The History of the Early Relations Between the United States and China, 1784-1844.* New Haven: Connecticut Academy of Arts & Sciences/Yale University Press, 1917.

Ljungstedt, Anders (also Sir Andrew). *An Historical Sketch of the Portuguese Settlements in China and of the Roman Catholic Church & Mission in China.* Boston: J. Munroe & Co., 1836.

Morison, Samuel Eliot. *The Maritime History of Massachusetts.* Boston: Houghton Mifflin Company, 1921.

Oberholtzer, Ellis Paxson. *Robert Morris, Patriot and Financier.* New York: Macmillan & Co., 1903.

Osgood, Charles Stuart, and Henry Morrill Batchelder. *Historical Sketch of Salem, 1626.* Salem: Essex Institute, 1879.

Peabody, Robert Ephraim. *Merchant Venturers of Old Salem.* Boston: Houghton Mifflin Company, 1912.

Quincy, Josiah. *The Journals of Major Samuel Shaw, the First American Consul at Canton; with a Life of the Author.* Boston: W. Crosby and H. P. Nichols, 1847.

Sainsbury, Ethel Bruce. *A Calendar of the Court Minutes, etc., of the East India Company, 1668-1670.* With an introduction and notes by Sir William Foster. Oxford: The Clarendon Press, 1929.

Sparks, Jared. *The Life of John Ledyard, the American Traveller.* Boston: C. C. Little and J. Brown, 1847.

Staunton, Sir George Leonard, 1st Bart., comp. *An Authentic Account of an Embassy from the King of Great Britain to the*

Emperor of China. . . Taken from the Papers of His Excellency the Earl of Macartney. London: G. Nicol, 1797.

Staunton, Sir George Thomas, Bart. *Miscellaneous Notes Relating to China, and Our Commercial Intercourse with That Country, Including a Few Translations from the Chinese Language.* London: J. Murray, 1822.

Williams, S[amuel] Wells. *The Middle Kingdom, a Survey of the Geography, Government, Education, Social Life, Arts, Religion, etc., of the Chinese Empire and its Inhabitants,* vol. 2. New York and London: Wiley & Putnam, 1848.

B. *Other works of interest*
(*C = exhibition catalog*)

Alexander, William, and George Henry Mason. *Views of 18th Century China—Costumes: History: Customs.* London: Studio Editions, 1988.

Beeching, Jack. *The Chinese Opium Wars.* New York and London: Harcourt Brace Jovanovich, 1975.

Berry-Hill, Henry and Sidney. *Chinnery and China Coast Paintings.* Leigh-on-Sea, 1970.

——. *George Chinnery, 1774-1852: Artist of the China Coast.* Leigh-on-Sea, 1963.

Carswell, John, with contributions by Edward A. Mason and Jean McClure Mudge. *Blue and White: Chinese Porcelain and Its Impact on the Western World.* Chicago: The David and Alfred Smart Gallery of the University of Chicago, 1985 (*C*).

Cary, Thomas G. *Memoir of Thomas Handasyd Perkins; containing extracts from his Diaries and Letters.* Boston: Little, Brown and Company, 1856.

The Chinese Traveller, Containing a Geographical, Commercial, and Political History of China. London: Braddon and Brodderice, c. 1800.

Chinnery & the China Coast: Paintings from the Collection of The Hongkong and Shanghai Bank. With introductory notes by Nigel Cameron. Hong Kong: The Hongkong and Shanghai Banking Corporation Limited, 1990. (*C*).

Christman, Margaret C. S. *Adventurous Pursuits: Americans and the China Trade, 1784-1844.* Washington: Smithsonian Institution Press, 1984. (*C*).

Clunas, Craig, ed. *Chinese Export Art and Design.* London: Victoria and Albert Museum, 1987 *(C).*

Crossman, Carl L. *The China Trade: Export Paintings, Furniture, Silver and Other Objects.* With a Foreword by Ernest S. Dodge. Princeton: The Pyne Press, 1972. (New edition in preparation, to be published by the Antique Collectors Club, Woodbridge, Suffolk, England.)

Davis, Sir John Francis, Bart., F.R.S. *China, During the War and Since the Peace.* 2 vols. London: Longman, Brown, Green, and Longmans, 1852.

——. *The Chinese: A General Description of the Empire of China and its Inhabitants.* 2 vols. New York: Harper & Brothers, 1836.

Denker, Ellen Paul. *After the China Taste: China's Influence in America, 1730-1930.* Salem: Peabody Museum of Salem, 1985. *(C).*

Fay, Peter Ward. *The Opium War: 1840-42.* New York and London: W. W. Norton & Company, 1976.

Feller, John Quentin. *The Canton Famille Rose Porcelains.* Salem: Peabody Museum of Salem, 1983 *(C).*

——. "Canton *famille rose* porcelain. Part I: Rose Medallion," *The Magazine ANTIQUES,* CXXIV, 4 (October 1983), pp. 748-758.

——. "Canton *famille rose* porcelain. Part II: Mandarin," *The Magazine ANTIQUES,* CXXV, 2 (February 1984), pp. 444-453.

——. "Canton *famille rose* porcelain. Part III: The flower patterns," *The Magazine ANTIQUES,* CXXVII, 1 (January 1985), pp. 284-291.

——. "Canton *famille rose* porcelain. Part IV: Some rare and unusual pieces," *The Magazine ANTIQUES,* CXXX, 4 (October 1986), pp. 722-731.

——. *The Society of the Cincinnati, 1783-1983.* Salem: Peabody Museum of Salem, 1983. *(C).*

Forbes, H. A. Crosby, John Devereux Kernan and Ruth S. Wilkins. *Chinese Export, Silver, 1785 to 1885.* Milton, Mass.: Museum of the American China Trade, 1975.

Goldstein, Jonathan. *Philadelphia and the China Trade, 1682-1846.* University Park and London: The Pennsylvania State University Press, 1978.

Gray, James. *Walks in the Streets of Canton.* London: 1875.

Hao, Yen-P'ing. *The Comprador in Nineteenth Century China: Bridge Between East and West.* Cambridge: Harvard University Press, 1970.

Hickey, William. *Memoirs 1745-1809.* 4 vols. London: Hurst and Blackett, 1925.

Howard, David Sanctuary, with an essay by Conrad Edick Wright. *New York and the China Trade.* New York: The New-York Historical Society, 1984 *(C).*

Irving, Washington. *Astoria.* Lincoln and London: University of Nebraska Press, 1982 (published by arrangement with G. K. Hall & Company, Boston).

Jewitt, John R. *The Adventures and Sufferings of John R. Jewitt, Captive of Maquinna,* annot. and illus. by Hilary Stewart. Seattle: The University of Washington Press, 1987.

——. *Captive of the Nootka Indians: the Northwest Coast Adventure of John R. Jewitt, 1802-1806.* Illus. by artists of the expeditions of Captain James Cook (1778) and of Alejandro Malaspina (1791). Ed. by Alice W. Shurcliff. (In preparation; to be published by Northeastern University Press, Boston.)

Johnson, Robert Erwin. *Far China Station: The U. S. Navy in Asian Waters, 1800-1898.* Annapolis: Naval Institute Press, 1979.

Lee, Jean Gordon, with an essay by Philip Chadwick Foster Smith. *Philadelphians and the China Trade, 1784-1844.* Philadelphia: Philadelphia Museum of Art, 1984 *(C).*

Lockwood, Stephen C. *Augustine Heard and Company: 1858-1862. American Merchants in China.* Cambridge: Harvard University Press, 1971.

Mudge, Jean McClure. *Chinese Export Porcelain in North America.* New York: Clarkson N. Potter, Inc./Publishers, 1986.

Nelson, Christina H. *Directly from China: Export Goods for the American Market, 1784-1930.* Salem: Peabody Museum of Salem, 1984. *(C).*

Palmer, Arlene. *A Winterthur Guide to Chinese Export Porcelain.* New York: Crown Publishers, 1976.

Schiffer, Herbert, Peter and Nancy. *China for America: Export Porcelain of the 18th and 19th Centuries.* Exton, Penn.: Schiffer Publishing Ltd., 1980.

Seaburg, Carl, and Stanley Paterson. *Merchant Prince of Boston: Colonel T. H. Perkins, 1764-1854.* Cambridge: Harvard University Press, 1971.

Stackpole, Edouard A. *Captain Prescott and the Opium Smugglers.* Mystic, Conn.: The Marine Historical Association, Inc., 1954.

Tamarin, Alfred, and Shirley Glubok. *Voyaging to Cathay: Americans in the China Trade.* New York: The Viking Press, 1976.

Tiffany, Osmond, Jr., *The Canton Chinese, or the American's Sojourn in the Celestial Empire.* Boston and Cambridge: James Monroe and Co., 1849.

Tillotson, G. H. R. *Fan Kwae Pictures: Paintings and Drawings by George Chinnery and Other Artists in the Collection of The Hongkong and Shanghai Banking Corporation.* London: Spink & Son Ltd., 1987.

Trevor-Roper, Hugh. *The Hermit of Peking: The Hidden Life of Sir Edmund Backhouse.* New York: Alfred A. Knopf, 1977.

Valenstein, Suzanne G. *A Handbook of Chinese Ceramics.* Rev. and enl. ed. New York: The Metropolitan Museum of Art/Harry N. Abrams, Inc., 1989.

Vollmer, John E. *In the Presence of the Dragon Throne: Ch'ing Dynasty Costume (1644-1911).* Toronto: Royal Ontario Museum, 1977 (C).

Vollmer, John E., E. J. Keall and E. Nagai-Berthrong. *Silk Roads—China Ships.* Toronto: Royal Ontario Museum, 1983 (C).

INDEX

DOROTHY SCHURMAN HAWES was born in Ithaca, New York, in 1905, the youngest of seven children of Barbara Forrest Munro Schurman and Jacob Gould Schurman, president of Cornell University. (After his retirement from Cornell in 1920, her father served as U. S. minister to China, 1921-25, and ambassador to Germany, 1925-30. Earlier in his career, he had chaired an American commission to investigate local conditions in the newly-acquired Philippine Islands, in 1899, and had been minister to Greece and Montenegro, 1912-13.)

Dorothy was educated at Rosemary Hall School and Bryn Mawr College. In 1926 she married a young Marine Corps officer, James Marshall McHugh, with whom she was to live for ten years in Shanghai and Beijing. Her husband served there as a regimental officer and naval attaché, and was the personal representative of the secretary of the navy to Generalissimo Chiang Kai-shek. He was the author of a textbook on China and a Chinese-English dictionary. Their marriage ended in divorce, and she was later married to Robert Nicholas Hawes and to James Strother Sisk. She was the mother of four children.

In addition to the present work, she was the author of a monograph on her ancestor, "William Schurman, Loyalist," published in the *Quarterly Bulletin of the Westchester County Historical Society* in 1932. She died in Purcellville, Virginia, in 1977.

JOHN QUENTIN FELLER, Ph.D., is professor of history at the University of Scranton and a trustee and honorary curator of Chinese export porcelain at the Peabody Museum of Salem. A member of the American Ceramic Circle, he has written extensively on export porcelain in various journals such as *Antiques* and *Winterthur Portfolio*. He is the author of *Chinese Export Porcelain in the Nineteenth Century* and, more recently, of *Dorflinger: America's Finest Glass, 1852-1921*. He lectures frequently on porcelain and glass throughout the United States.

Description of cover illustrations. (Photographs by George Pugh.)

Front cover:

The Factories at Canton, c. 1850. This gouache, almost certainly painted by Tingqua, records the appearance of Canton between May 1847, when a plot of land for the new Protestant church was purchased, and December 1856, when the factories were deliberately fired by the Chinese as a reprisal for a British naval attack. 7-1/4 in. X 11 in. (Collection of John Quentin Feller.)

Back cover — examples of Chinese export porcelain:

(1) *Dessert plate, 1870.* Decorated in the popular Rose Medallion pattern, this Canton *famille-rose* plate is part of a 158-piece dinner set ordered by Capt. Bushrod Bennett Taylor which, according to the bill of lading at the Peabody Museum, was shipped from Hong Kong aboard *Golden Fleece* on July 8, 1870. Diameter, 7-7/8 in. (Collection of John Quentin Feller.)

(2) *Pistol-handled urn, c. 1830.* This brilliantly painted vase, one of a pair, is in the Canton *famille-rose* pattern known as Mandarin, and was exactly the sort of decorative object which was specially ordered at the height of the "old China trade," i.e., prior to 1842. Overall height, 16-1/4 in. (Collection of John Quentin Feller, on loan to the Peabody Museum of Salem.)

(3) *Reticulated underdish, c. 1850.* This colorful Canton *famille-rose* dish originally sat under a matching oval fruit bowl, and is decorated in the Garden pattern. Length, 9-1/2 in. (Collection of John Quentin Feller, on loan to the Peabody Museum of Salem.)